REBEL CHURCH

REBEL CHURCH

A challenge and an encouragement

to the Believer

PETER SAMMONS

Glory to Glory Publications

First published in Great Britain in 2013 by
Glory to Glory Publications, an imprint of Buy Research Ltd.
Glory to Glory Publications
PO Box 212 SAFFRON WALDEN CB10 2UU

ISBN 978-0-9926674-0-5

Printed by Imprint Digital, Exeter

Contents

Foreword

If the Christian message is anything, it is one of profound good news, of a God intimately involved in the trials of His people, and who has given His Son to be a complete remedy to mankind's continual rebellion. The good news is that ultimately the future is God's future! And yet the good news is not universally accepted – to some it is the fragrance of life, yet to others it is the stench of death (2 Corinthians 2:16).

There can be few Christians today unaware of the huge gulfs that are opening up within what we are pleased to call 'church' as regards belief and praxis. Broadly, there is a widening gulf separating those who choose to follow Jesus as Lord and Master, and those who choose the world's way, but who cover their choice with a fig leaf of Christian respectability.

There is an absolute responsibility on every believer to look first and foremost to their own spiritual health. Each of us must answer to God for our own sins – not the sins of others! If the church is unhealthy, must we as individual believers also suffer? Can we remain true as individuals even where the organised church is palpably false? This book demonstrates that the answer is 'yes'! If the church increasingly rejects biblical truth, then the individual believer remains answerable for where they stand. Hiding behind a vicar's cassock or a pastor's reputation will never be enough. Jesus warned of false gospels and false messiahs. Do we take His warnings seriously? Not all of the church is false – that is definitely not the message of this book – but Jesus said plainly that significant numbers of 'church people' (to use a modern term) would fail the ultimate test (Matthew 25). What sort of a Christian are you?

This book opens up a blessed opportunity for the individual believer to step more assuredly along the narrow road that leads to life (Matthew 7:14). A vision for the year AD 2020 and beyond is opened up. Where there is no vision, the people perish (Proverbs 29:18). Catch the vision!

Introduction

Why?

Jesus gave warnings that not all of His church would be ready for His return in glory. Indeed it is rightly said that most of the Lord Jesus' warnings about eternal loss and eternal punishment were not directed to the world at large, but to His church – to those who follow Him. As Jesus gave these warnings, it would be the height of folly not to heed them and ponder them.

I once asked a Christian artist how long it took him to paint his pictures. I was expecting him to say something like: "Forty hours for the big one over there, and twenty-five hours for the small one just here." But his answer was more nuanced – and, in a sense, more obvious. He said, "Peter, I don't mean to sound conceited, but it takes a lifetime to paint these pictures." What he meant was that the artist's style develops, changes and responds to life's experiences. So what he paints in 2014 is a product of what he was painting over the years 1970 to 2013.

It is the same with writing books, and especially Christian books. The things that concern me as a man of 55 are not (necessarily) the things that concerned me as a man of 25, but they are informed by the experiences of those intervening thirty years, as well as changes in the world – and, it must be said, changes in the church. In Hebrews 13:8 we read **Jesus, the Messiah, is the same yesterday and today — and forever!** (ISV 2012) We can say emphatically that Jesus is the same, and that His message and His call do not change, and that Kingdom ethics do not change. Nor, we might add, do our deepest human needs change. But the church *does* change, and Jesus' teaching includes warnings which help us to evaluate change.

Does Jesus want a static church, one that does not respond to – and engage with – the world and the cultures in which it lives? The Amish[1] community in America seem to think so. But there is little validity in any argument that Jesus thought this. Far from divorcing Himself from the world, our Lord was intimately involved in it, preaching and teaching that we should seek His *Kingdom* even while we are here in this world (Matthew 6:33). Jesus lived on earth and taught in a country occupied by a glowering foreign power. He knew of change in the past, and He foresaw change in the future. This book is not about a static church, nor is it a call to freeze-frame the church at a certain point in history, but in a sense it *is* about an unchanging church, one that is true to its message, one that is true to the Scriptures and one that is true to its Lord. One that is true to *the* Lord – who declared Himself to be *the Truth* (John 14:6).

In this book we will examine from a biblical viewpoint what Jesus says about His church, its mission and how it is to behave. We will also look at what Jesus says about the church in the end times. But this is not a book about the end times. There are many studies that have examined that subject and I do not intend to explore it in detail. This is a book that challenges the church at large to own up to what sort of church it is, and what sort of church it expects to develop into. And: what sort of Lord does the church seek to present and to represent in the present age? But even more it is for individual Christian believers: irrespective of 'the church', what sort of believer are you? Many ordinary Christians are today appalled at the 'evolution' of the church into an organisation that seems hell-bent on opposing the Holy Spirit. How are these individual Christians to respond

---

[1] Whether the Amish are Christians or a cult depends on your viewpoint. At a simple level they appear to hold to a theology of "Salvation by Works", something emphatically rejected in the Bible.

to the recalcitrant and frankly rebellious leaders who so often seem to be the denominationally appointed representatives of Jesus, as the official 'heads' of their churches?

Your author's thoughts in this whole subject have been influenced by events and teaching over the past thirty years. As the author of a book looking at religious syncretism and how it is infecting the church (*The Empty Promise of Godism*, Glory to Glory Publications, 2009) it was perhaps inevitable that I would revisit the subject of 'Whither the church?' – or *where is the church going*? And especially to revisit this question with a clear acknowledgement that indeed parts of the church are hell-bent on going their own way and are simply not going to change – ever. So what happens to faithful, concerned individual Christians in these situations? If they are certain that their church will not change, do they simply ride out the coming storms, clinging to the wreckage that was once the church family they knew and loved? Do they hope for the best? Do they continually switch churches in the hope of finding something better? Or do they do something entirely different? What does Jesus have to say? These questions are what we seek to address in the pages that follow.

I thought long and hard before including the following section but believe it is ultimately right to 'call a spade a spade'. Some of the symptoms of a church that has gone wrong are as follows:

• An 'Episcopalian' church Bishop (Paul Moore of New York) appeared with a female 'priest' on television, to support her. The 'priest' had artificially inseminated herself with the mixed sperm of three donors (two of them Episcopalian 'priests') because she wanted a baby but not a husband. Use of the sperm of three was to keep the father's identity veiled. Bishop Moore said "As her bishop I can affirm that which **** has done. I have no intention of disciplining her, criticising her or condemning her.... I don't see that she has in any way broken any of the commandments" (interview with *Washington Post*, reported in THE HOUR, Northwalk Conn on 12 December 1987, when the female 'priest' announced she was planning the same procedure a second time).

• Steve Chalke, a well known 'evangelical' minister in the UK, who in 2004 earned an MBE for his work on 'social inclusion', announced in 2003 in a book that he did not hold to the basic Reformed-evangelical understanding of the penal substitution of Christ for sinners. In a global and often 'broad' church, historically riven by theological controversies, this might be thought as quite unremarkable. So what? Nevertheless, such a view strikes at the foundation of the Cross. It was noteworthy that he later came out in favour of homosexual marriage. As long ago as 1992, Dr Martin Lloyd Jones wrote a short book entitled *What is an Evangelical?*, the thesis of which was to challenge the term 'evangelical' which even then was becoming a catch-all for those church people who were *enthusiastic Christians* but not necessarily Bible believing or otherwise authentic Christians.

Sadly, Chalke gave detractors of the Cross a wonderful new phrase – 'cosmic child abuse' – to undermine the truth that God transfers the punishment due to penitent sinners on to His own Son. This phrase tapped-in splendidly with a legitimate societal concern, that of various forms of child abuse, and so made the phrase instantly a media soundbite. Christians down through two millennia have clung to the wonderful truth in Romans 5:8 – that **God demonstrates his own love for us in this: while we were still sinners, Christ died for us**. And, further, that we are saved from God's wrath through Jesus (v. 9) **through whom we have**

been reconciled through His death. 2 Corinthians 5:21 speaks powerfully into this subject. The purpose of this book about the rebel church is not to resolve this controversy, but we are bound to note how the truth of the gospel is wilfully misrepresented by some. At the end of a high profile public debate on this subject, many clerics laughed at Chalke's humour and warmly applauded him, thus aligning with his *cosmic child abuse* theology. Some by contrast might consider this to be blasphemous.

• In Seattle USA, a female minister, Anne Holmes Redding, of the 'Episcopalian' church (a decidedly liberal manifestation of 'church') became a Muslim but saw no difficulty in continuing to officiate at her own church Sunday meetings. It took that church some three years of deliberation before deciding to defrock her. Again, at one level religious shenanigans among the religious may seem quite unremarkable, but the fact it took three years to reach and then effect a solution must be noteworthy in what might otherwise have been thought of as an open-and-shut case.

• Archbishop Rowan Williams, a former head of the global Anglican communion, apparently became a Druid – or at least actively engaged in a Druid ceremony. This led to the BBC-online headline 5 August 2002 of ***Archbishop Becomes a Druid*** (at time of writing this book the article is still online – just Google 'is archbishop a druid?'). The BBC report went on:

The new Archbishop of Canterbury has been inducted as a druid in a centuries-old Celtic ceremony. Dr Rowan Williams, the current Archbishop of Wales, said that he had been "saddened" by the misrepresentations about the ceremony, which sparked concern about pagan links. "Some people have reached the wrong conclusion about the ceremony," he said. "If people had actually looked at the words of the hymns and text used they would have seen a very Christian service."

Dr Williams became a member of the highest of the three orders of the Gorsedd of Bards – a 1,300-strong circle of Wales' key cultural contributors – in a ceremony at this year's National Eisteddfod celebration of Welsh culture in St Davids, Pembrokeshire. The ceremony, which took more than an hour, started with a procession from the main Eisteddfod Pavilion to a circle of stones on the edge of the site. Dr Williams, 52, wore a long white cloak without any headdress as he arrived at the back of the procession.

According to the BBC's National Eisteddfod 2011 website:

Gorsedd y Beirdd members are present on stage during three of the main Eisteddfod ceremonies dressed in their white, blue and green robes, being led by the Archdruid. The colours of the robes denote the different ranks. In the same way that the Gorsedd emblem has three shafts, the Gorsedd has three orders of merit:

1. *The Ovate Order – green robe, which includes the Bardic Ovate, the Musician Ovate and the Literature Ovate. Membership on passing the first two Gorsedd examinations. Honorary members on the recommendation of the Gorsedd Board in recognition of service to Wales.*

2. *The Order of Bards, Linguist, Musicians and Literati – blue robe. Membership of this Order can only be obtained on passing the final Gorsedd examination. Graduates who have been successful in Welsh and Welsh Literature, or Music, in their Final Examination may also apply.*

3. The Druidic Order – white robe. This order is restricted to those honoured by the Gorsedd Board for their substantial contribution to Literature, Music, Scholarship, Science or Arts in Wales. Green and blue robed members can be elevated to this order. Chief Bards and Prose Medal winners are also accepted to this order.

Whether the Archbishop was, or was not, a Druid may not be the essential issue in this case; he certainly appeared to be identifying wholeheartedly with a pagan religion. His prior selection by the Tony Blair government as senior prelate of the established church seemed to be in keeping with that party's desire to 'modernise' everything, including the church. The archbishop was later to stun the nation by apparently calling for parts of Islamic Shariah Law to be recognised and enforced in the UK.

• In June 2000 the UK Methodist Church appointed Reverend Inderjit Bhogal, a 46-year-old clergyman and theologian, as *President of the Conference*, a one-year appointment that made him the titular head of Methodism. The role is as close as Methodism's hierarchy gets to an Archbishop. What type of 'Christian' he was/is may be open to question. What is not open to question is his commitment to interfaith 'dialogue' (for which he received an OBE) and his view that all religions have merit. At the very least this is a questionable viewpoint. In one online blog Bhogal described himself as a "Methodist with strong roots in Sikhism", thus making unclear his exclusive discipleship of Jesus, or of what sort of Jesus he actually believed in. The Methodist church globally now has a reputation for extreme liberalism and an apparent penchant for syncretism.

• Over the years 2009–13 The Rev Glynn Cardy in Auckland NZ arranged for a series of posters to be bill-boarded outside his large Anglican church. In 2009 his poster depicted a cartoon of Mary and Joseph in bed, looking glum and with the banner 'Poor Joseph. God was a hard act to follow.' A second poster depicted the Virgin Mary looking shocked at the result of a pregnancy test. In December 2012 the church's poster was of an infant Jesus in a crib with a rainbow halo around his head and the banner headline 'Its Christmas. Time for Jesus to come out' – a reference to homosexuality. At Easter 2013, to 'cleverly' link with Pope Benedict XVI's resignation, a poster depicted the crucified Jesus with the banner 'Is resigning an option?' What is perhaps most disturbing about such shenanigans, is that a church community will continue to support it, and continue to receive spiritual oversight from such leadership.

• A minister in a UK 'Protestant' denomination told the author that when making at a keynote speech within his denomination about the subject of homosexuality from a biblical perspective, as he moved to the platform to make his speech he was hissed by a large sub-section of the other ministers present.

• The author received an email from a minister in one of the smaller UK denominations in which he stated that he did not believe in original sin, and that he considered all religions, including paganism, were acceptable to God. Theologically this would be called universalism. When I mentioned the email to another minister in the same denomination, he smiled faintly: "Ah yes," he said, "the Rev **** and his husband are well known within the denomination for their rather eccentric views!"

• The author once met a Baptist minister who had taught for a term at a theological seminary in the USA. Whilst interviewing the students preparing for ministry, several were emphatic that in practice they did not actually believe in God. When he asked them why they wanted to become church ministers, their story was that they wanted to do 'good works' and thought that the Baptist church would facilitate this ambition. He told me that he encouraged them to think of another career. The alarming thing is that candidates for ministry (a) should have got that far and (b) could not easily be discharged from their theology course. As the minister who mentioned this story left the seminary shortly afterwards, he did not know whether the students went on to become accredited ministers.

• The tragic stories of 'priestly abuse' emerging from Roman Catholic Church suggests there is a yawning gap between professed faith and practice. It is true that there are controversies within the Orthodox tradition (Russian and Greek varieties), although in fairness most of these are completely different in nature to those suggested above.

• The week this book was begun (in June 2013), an Anglican 'priest' in the UK placed on YouTube a video of her officiating at a wedding – ending the ceremony with a 'Flashmob' dance, choreographed with family and friends. The video went viral and the vicar was on television a few days later. She had bridged the gap between religion and entertainment, surely setting a precedent. Since the relationship between Christ and His church is that of bridegroom and bride, there is a holiness, an otherness and a mystery around the ordinance and holy estate of marriage that has always been seen as serious. We speak of solemnising a marriage with good reason. Whilst the Bible makes no specific demands around the physical characteristics of a wedding ceremony, it does treat marriage with the utmost seriousness. The secular media were delighted in June 2013. A vicar in their own mould?

These are just a few samples of the way that the organised church has developed in recent years. Whilst the examples given are largely UK or US ones, there is no doubt that similar convulsions are impacting all the so-called 'denominations' around the world. Of course there has always been a struggle between 'liberal' and moderating forces within the church, between those who wish to hold fast to biblical truths and those who want to move away from them. Such struggles were both encountered and are prefigured in the New Testament. Accordingly they should not be a surprise to us. The apostle Paul warned of a time in the future when people would gather around themselves a certain type of teacher. When Paul spoke of 'people' the context makes it reasonably certain that he meant people *within* the church – although it is likely that the world at large will connive in this. Paul wrote: **For the time will come when people will not put up with sound doctrine. Instead, to suit their own desires, they will gather around them a great number of teachers to say what their itching ears want to hear** (2 Timothy 4:3). The task for the believing Christian has always been to understand the time in which they live and to be aware of – and frankly to be wary of – teachers who dilute the gospel message.

The purpose of this book is not to resolve the contro-versies, theological or otherwise, that afflict the church. The purpose of this book is not, by the same token, to promote one type of theology over others in the hope that it may be more widely accepted. No, the purpose of this book is to acknowledge that there has always been, is today, and always will be, a rebel church, whilst also facing up to the fact that rebel forces will increase and will grow more powerful in what the Bible calls the end times. Jesus called upon His disciples to read the signs of the times. His warnings are given precisely with the understanding that we are to be aware of – and be wise to – what is going on. Accordingly, if you are a disciple of the Lord Jesus, you need to make a decision as to where you are going to stand. The church to which you adhere today may be a very different church tomorrow.

Whilst providing awareness, this book will seek to help Christians to map out a course that *will* take them closer to their Lord, to experience Him more deeply, and to consciously build themselves up for the battles that certainly lie ahead. In that sense this book seeks to be a starting point in a journey aimed at knowing the Lord Jesus better and placing ourselves more firmly on His path and on His agenda. For Jesus *does* have an agenda for our times and for our days.

Who?

For whom is this book written? Who does the author think are his likely readers?

The book is written specifically for one group – disciples who love Jesus as Lord and as Saviour and who know that the church that bears His name is no longer completely true to Him. Jesus said "**my sheep listen to my voice**" (John 10:27). The sheep in any flock come to know the authentic voice of their shepherd. They will listen out for and follow that voice, which leads them to sustenance and to safety. They will be rightly suspicious of other voices. Jesus spoke about 'hired hands' – shepherds who were only working for a wage, who will abandon the sheep (John 10:12) when it seems right to them to do so. We would be foolish to assume that these are just throw-away lines from our Lord. He spoke them for a reason. Christians are only to follow His true voice. This is not to suggest that Christians will be monotone, template cut-outs, all looking the same, thinking the same and doing the same things. For reasons we will explore later in this book, that is emphatically not what Jesus is looking for. But there comes a point at which the beliefs of some churches and church leaders depart so markedly from revealed biblical truth that they cease to be authentic expressions of Christianity. Those who hold heretical beliefs know in their hearts that they are far away from Jesus. Christians who are disturbed by what they see and experience in such 'rebel' churches are those for whom this book is primarily written, with the prayer that it will help them to know what is true, recognise what is false and respond appropriately.

Some who are avowedly 'liberal' in in their thinking may pick up this book, if only to find ways to counter it. If you are one of those readers, then you are more than welcome. The challenge for you is to try with honesty and integrity to listen to the authentic voice of Jesus, who is known to believers as Master, Saviour, Messiah, Son of God, Lord and God (John 20:28). And whatever the author of *Rebel Church* writes should be compared by the reader against what the Bible teaches, and, where any conflict may be found, it is the plain teaching of the Bible that should be believed.

Some on the fringes of cultic belief, such as Mormons and Jehovah's Witnesses, may also be intrigued by what is explored in this study.

Finally, those of what the author has elsewhere referred to as 'the religions' might stumble across this book and sense that Jesus may be able to speak into their own situation. They also might perceive a church that appears in places to be completely adrift from its core values, and may wonder how this could possibly be, and may ponder what sort of God tolerates behaviour that can only be described as rebellious. Has this God been duped, or has He all along foreseen rebellion and fixed in place remedies and precisely prefigured outcomes?

It is most unlikely that atheists will read this book, unless again they are seeking ammunition to fire back at believers. If you are an atheist or an agnostic then you have two options – put down the book now and find another way to spend your next few evenings, or read on in the hope that you will get at least two worthwhile benefits: first, you will better understand the attitude of Jesus to the church that bears His name; second, you may acquire a better appreciation of normative biblical Christianity.

How?

The author recognises that most readers will approach this book with limited knowledge of the Bible – and some with absolutely no knowledge whatsoever. And sadly this includes many professing Christians. These readers can have confidence that in working through this book they will pick up a little 'head knowledge' along the way. Whilst this is not going to be a crash course on the Bible or on theology, inevitably readers will pick up some understanding of the Bible as they follow the argument. In this introduction we will, however, make three simple observations about the Bible, so readers can get a clear sense of how the author approaches the subject:

1. The Bible is divided into Old and New Testaments

This immediately sounds rather obscure and the author acknowledges that these titles and divisions are not altogether helpful. The Old Testament tells especially of the dealings of God through His chosen people – the Hebrews. The New Testament tells of God's dealings with humankind through Jesus, His Son, whom His followers called "Lord" as they acknowledged Him to have ultimate control over their lives. The two Testaments are therefore pre-Messianic and post-Messianic. Old Testament and New Testament might better be thought of as "The Promise" (for the Old Testament) and "The Promise Fulfilled" (for the New Testament). This at least recognises that the Old reveals God's insistent promise that He will one day send a Saviour to the world, whilst the New reveals who that Saviour is – Jesus the Messiah. But even these titles are not altogether helpful, as some of the promises of the Old Testament (and indeed some promises in the New Testament) have yet to be fulfilled in the future. But, even so, try to hold on to the thought of *promise* and *promise fulfilled* as you work through this book. The idea at least provides one context in which to think about the 66 books that make up the Bible and the way the two "Testaments" stand in relation to each other. They are interconnected in very many ways – the New does not replace the Old, it confirms it. *Hand in glove* might be a better analogy for the way these two 'Testaments' relate to each other.

Another way of looking at the two testaments has been suggested by some theologians. They say that the word 'testament' actually means 'covenant' and what the phrases show us is that the 'old covenant' is replaced by the 'new covenant'. This is wrong at a number of levels but seems to have some currency in popular theological thinking. I would venture that the word 'testament' as traditionally applied to the two main parts of the Bible (the pre-Messianic and the post-Messianic) actually means – testament! The historically reliable usage of the word 'testament' was always that the Old Testament bore witness to the coming Messiah whilst the New Testament bore witness to who that Messiah actually is (Jesus) and set in place the outworking of God's final purposes for all mankind. Think of it in this way: where a bank is robbed and people see what happened, they are called eye-witnesses. When they come to court as witnesses for the prosecution, the story they tell is called their testimony. So in the same way, down through history there were many witnesses to God's outworking of His purposes both before the time of Jesus, during His earthly ministry and then during the apostolic church period. Hence it is in some sense correct to refer to these biblical accounts as 'testimonies'.

The term 'Testament', at least by this way of thinking, is correct and helpful.

Whilst for the purposes of this book we will use both Testaments to explore God's heart in the subject under consideration, and its primary focus is on the rebellious church, it will be understood that our primary 'document-ation' must be the New Testament. The New Testament describes in detail the earthly ministry of Jesus and the establishing of his church. It is in the New Testament that virtually all the warnings of falsehood within the professing assembly of Christians are contained, and where the guidance for Christians in how to deal with these situations is most explicit. Whilst Old Testament principles certainly do speak into these situations, it is within the New Testament that the focus becomes crystal clear.

2. Is the Bible dependable?

Let us just consider its dependability for a moment. In this book we take if as foundational but do not seek to *prove here by argument* that the Holy Scriptures are the definitive word of God. There are many good books that examine the Holy Bible in that context and no doubt someone who is genuinely interested in this subject will readily find what they need without having to look too hard. If the reader comes to this book with the objection that the Bible *is not*, or *may not be*, the sole revelation of 'god' then he or she is invited simply to 'park' that objection for the time being. There surely can be no great problem in looking closely at what the Scriptures have to say about the church and its future, so as to acquire a clear understanding of the argument being put forward in this book.

In a court of law, as each witness gives their testimony, a judge and jury will form an opinion as to the trustworthiness of that particular person, and the validity of the testimony they offer. The author invites his readers to adopt the same attitude towards the Bible. Readers can always 'call more witnesses' at a later stage if they feel that the witness of Scripture is incomplete or invalid. The key suggestion made by this author is that a doubter proceeds from this point onwards with the basic working assumption that the Scriptures *are* valid and trustworthy. That provides the platform from which to review what Jesus says to us about this question of a rebel church.

Allowing that many readers will be Westerners, then we might as well also 'park' the gender issue too: some may feel that reference to God as 'Him' and 'He' represents some form of gender aggression. We use those terms because the Bible does. You can always return to that question and examine it later.

3. Precisely how should we read the Bible?

In essence the way most serious Christians read the Bible is to take the text at its plainest and simplest meaning – in other words, in the way the writer clearly meant the words to be read and understood. We should only read the text in another way if it is quite obvious that the writer or the context demands that it be read differently. That is the approach adopted in this book. Christians believe that God, the Creator (or 'Maker') has given us the *maker's instructions*. If we ignore them we do so at our peril. If the Maker has given instructions and warnings, isn't it wise and prudent to make an effort to understand them? That's what we set out to do in this book, using the Bible as our guide.

Throughout, we will quote, sometimes extensively, from the Bible. Readers are invited to judge *Rebel Church*, and in a sense its author, on the basis of whether the extracts used are true to the spirit of the Bible as a whole, and true to the context in which the verses were originally given. It has been rightly said that *a verse taken out of context is a pretext*. In other words there are people who will take parts of the Bible and use them in ways never intended by God, whom the Scriptures tell us is the ultimate author of the Bible. People may take verses right out of context and use them as a pretext to support some factional viewpoint. Wherever possible, and where it does not needlessly disrupt the flow of the argument being developed, we will try to give a sense of the context in which the Scripture portions used in this book were likely to have been understood by the first readers back in biblical times. The referencing system used in this book is always book, chapter and verse in the following typical format: Psalm chapter 34 verse 8 would be rendered: Psalm 34:8.

Signs of the Times
Matthew 5:13 – **You are the salt of the earth. But if the salt loses its saltiness, how can it be made salty again? It is no longer good for anything, except to be thrown out and trampled by men**.
The Lord Jesus gave a number of sober warnings to His followers that they might lose their right to witness for Him.

Whether this necessarily involves losing their salvation is still keenly debated. The verse above, repeated in Mark 9:50 and Luke 14:34, is given in the context of discipleship. Salt was greatly valued in biblical times. Roman soldiers might receive their wages in salt. The Mosaic Law required that all offerings presented by the Israelites contain salt (Leviticus 2:13). When Jesus told His disciples that they were "the salt of the earth", they understood the simile. The mandate that Jesus gave to His first disciples remains applicable and relevant to His followers today. 'Salt of the earth' is no mean title: we should be amazed that Jesus elevates and honours his followers with this epithet. Salt had two key uses in the ancient world. First (as today) it is the primary food flavouring. Any cook knows they do not need to add much salt to transform a dish. In the same way, a little Christian salt can transform societies, as historically the prison reform movements, anti-slavery campaigns and free-school enterprises all demonstrate. Christians can and should, and generally do, 'flavour' their societies to make them better places. Society will not always collaborate with that task and may try to throw into the mix other dominating flavours, but salt usually seasons the underlying experience of the dish. Second, salt was – and remains – the great natural preservative. Without refrigeration, fish or meat will quickly spoil and rot unless they are packed in salt. Once salted, food can be safely stored and used when needed. One spiritual task of the Christian is to counteract the corruption of sin that dominates this world. Christians, as salt, are to inhibit sin from destroying lives and from destroying societies. This in turn creates opportunity for the gospel to be proclaimed and received.

There are other aspects to salt that theologians ponder: some believe that Christians are to sting the world with rebuke and judgment as the way salt stings an open wound. Others think that its whiteness represents the purity of the justified believer. It is suggested that, as salt, Christians are to create a thirst for Christ. Whilst all these ideas may have some element of truth, it is the preservative role that would have been one of the most immediate in the understanding of the disciples. Jesus' great affirmation comes with a stark warning, however. If salt loses its saltiness, how can that be restored? It is no longer good for anything, except to be thrown out and trodden underfoot. This must be a stark warning for the church. Once it ceases to be truly Christian, once it compromises with the world, once it engages in sin and indeed promotes sin, does it have anything of worth left? If it wins the world's plaudits, it may do so for only a short time. A church that reneges on the gospel will not be respected by the world – rather the opposite. With its irreverence it will become an irrelevance. Society will recognise this and ultimately will trample on what is left of that compromised church. Not so the remnant, however. The Lord Jesus will always keep a remnant alive, literally and metaphorically, until the very end, when the world will have its brief moment of apparent triumph over the church.[2]

Ultimately, and above any other consideration, it is what Jesus Himself thinks of a church that claims to bear His name, that matters – and that has eternal consequence.

This book seeks to alert true Christians to the issues at stake, to encourage wavering Christians and to map out strategies that will bring themselves as individuals, if not the wider 'organised church', back onto the narrow way that leads, if it is trodden faithfully, inevitably to life – and to life in all its fullness. No wonder Christians love their God, who has not withheld even His own dear Son but has given Him, **"that whosoever believes on Him"** and goes on believing on Him, will have eternal life, beginning in this world.

As we noted in the first paragraph in this Introduction, Jesus gave warnings – *certain* warnings – that not all of His church would be ready for His return in glory. Most of the Lord Jesus' warnings about eternal loss and eternal punishment were not directed to the world at large, but to His church – to those who claim to follow Him. As Jesus gave these warnings, it would be the height of folly not to heed and ponder them. Are you prepared to heed these warnings? And to what sort of church do you belong? A faithful church, or a rebel church?

Suffolk, England 2013

"Happy are those who have been invited to the wedding feast of the Lamb."

---

[2] It is helpful to note that, whilst the world will have its brief moment of triumph over the church, it will never triumph over the Kingdom – see chapter 1 for more thoughts on this distinction.

Chapter One

THE KINGDOM AND THE CHURCH

So what is the Church?

As the subject of this book is the *rebel church*, it is important we have real clarity in understanding what is, in fact, the 'church'. And this in turn will require a brief look at the mission of the Lord Jesus. In the UK (and perhaps elsewhere) we often tend to think of the church as being a building or an administrative organisation. Both ideas are wrong. A church is a group or assembly of people *called* together. The term appears only twice in the Gospels (i.e. in the life histories of Jesus – Matthew, Mark, Luke and John) in Matthew 16:18 and Matthew 18:17. The use of this word in the New Testament is influenced by similar or equivalent words in the Old Testament. In the latter the word used is designated as *the assembly of the Israelites*, particularly where they were gathered before God or hearing the Law (Deuteronomy 4:10; 16:8; 18:16; 31:30. Leviticus 4:14. Numbers 10:3, Judges 20:2, Acts 7:38). In Christian use within the New Testament a similar word is used.

A true believer in, and follower of, Jesus is always called by God whenever possible to relate closely to other believers. Forming communities of such believers where there can be a proper commitment to proclaiming the gospel, prayer, praise, baptism, sharing Holy Communion (breaking of bread/Eucharist) and maintaining a loving fellowship in the power of the Holy Spirit is the foundation for the biblical understanding of church. The word 'church' is the standard translation of the Greek word 'ecclesia' (literally 'called-out assembly'), used 112 times in the New Testament and, as stated, usually translated as 'church', but in some translations a term signifying 'congregation, place of worship, meeting or assembly' is used. In James 2:2 the Greek word is not 'ecclesia' but Synagogue, which is a helpful reminder to us that the early followers of Jesus were mainly Jewish. Many Bible translations get this wrong, using a non-Jewish sounding word instead.

The Bible uses several illustrations to explore the meaning of the church:

* It is, like the Israelites coming out of Egypt, a *chosen people* (1 Peter 2:9; Acts 7:38).
* It is like a *human body*, with its many different functions. (1 Corinthians 12:12–27; Ephesians 5:29–30).
* It is like a *holy temple*, made up of different precious stones, in which Jesus dwells. (1 Corinthians 3:16–17; Ephesians 32:21–22; 1 Peter 2:5).
* It is like a *bride* in a true love marriage where Jesus Himself is the husband. (Ephesians 5:28–30, Revelation 21:2 and 21:9).
* It is similar to a *virgin*, betrothed to Jesus. (Matthew 25:1–13; 2 Corinthians 11:2–3; Revelation 19:7).

The church, then, is the community of true believers and followers of Jesus. This includes both those believers living today and those who have died and are now with God in glory. It is better to think of the church as a living organism rather than as an institution, building or organisation – although every church must have some level of organisational structure and leadership. Seeking structure and leadership is thoroughly biblical and enables community life to flourish by making sure that all things are done in decency and order (see 1 Corinthians 14:40).

Sadly, the one true universal[1] and apostolic[2] church in the world today is divided into numerous denominations and groupings. While there are many historical, theological and pragmatic reasons for this, it does appear to work strongly against the desire of Jesus for true unity amongst His disciples (John 17:6-26). In God's ongoing purposes there is a clear link between unity and effective mission. True unity in faithfulness to Jesus and His Word, which all Christians should seek to pursue and maintain, should not be confused with uniformity in external structures of organisation, or styles of worship.

We can summarise by affirming that the true church consists of genuine disciples of Jesus, and He is their Head. This leads on to a further need for a definition. What is a *disciple* of Jesus – indeed what is a *Christian*, and are the two terms the same? Theologically speaking, a Christian is someone who has received the Lord Jesus as Saviour (John 1:12), trusts Him alone for the forgiveness of sins (Acts 4:12), has put no trust in his own efforts to please God (Isaiah 64:6), and has repented of his/her sins (Mark 1:15). A working definition could start like this: *to be a Christian means to believe and follow Christ, to desire Him, to fellowship with Him, to be indwelt by His Spirit, and to bring glory to Him in your life.* The terms 'Christian' and 'disciple' should in reality be entirely interchangeable – but in practice they are not! As was explored a little in the Introduction to this book, the various persons mentioned as symbolic of the current malaise within the broad church would no doubt style themselves 'Christians' – and would be recognised by the world as such. However, are they such, when assessed by a consistent and considered biblical understanding? That is no doubt a question for those individuals to answer, rather than for this writer to second-guess.

---

[1] The term 'catholic' in the creeds refers to the *universal* nature of the church
[2] The term 'apostolic' in the creeds refers to the fact that the church is built upon the faithful foundations of the apostles

In English the word *disciple* comes from the same root as the word *discipline*. A true Christian is a person who accepts the Lordship of Jesus and accordingly accepts His discipline, not seeking to argue with Him or overturn His revealed will, but seeking humbly to follow Him obediently. It is humility (or lack of humility) that may throw up the earliest question as to where a man or woman truly stands before the Lord. Of course Uriah Heep in Charles Dickens' novel *David Copperfield* has gone down in history as the archetypal man who claimed extreme humility but who was in fact a schemer out to get his own way! Appearances can be deceptive! There is one other aspect of the true Christian, the true disciple of Jesus which we have not yet touched upon, but will now remedy: a disciple of Jesus is a person who actively seeks the kingdom of God.

Writer Mike Endicott, in his powerful and entirely helpful short book *Kingdom Seekers*,[3] makes the point that *the kingdom is a place we are to seek*: "What we might call the kingdom of Christ it not somewhere that the kingdom seeker can come across by accident, nor a place to be discovered by his own unaided efforts. Neither is there any 'religious trick' that will turn the lock in the door. We are not called to find the kingdom but to seek it. It is in the seeking, rather than the finding, where we begin to discover the knowledge and benefits of kingdom living. The nature of this holy life is revealed to kingdom seekers through their asking; they will only find it by diligently seeking for it, and the door will be opened to those who knock."[4] Endicott goes on to point out that kingdom seekers try to live their lives centred on His kingdom: "We become wholly centred on the King. By uniting with him in our heart, will and spirit, we are united to all that He is and has in Himself. This is the holiness and perfection of living that we pray for in the Lord's Prayer – *that God's kingdom may come and His will be done in us*,

---

[3] *Kingdom Seekers* by Mike Endicott (Glory to Glory Publications, 2009).
[4] *Ibid*. p. 99

as it is in heaven. This is a discoverable place of reality. If it were not so, our Saviour would hardly have made it part of our daily prayer." [5]

So kingdom seeking is a real and a key task for the true believer. We will shortly turn to look at the Kingdom in a little more detail. To conclude our review of what is the church, we turn to Rev Patrick Whitworth's useful book *Becoming a Citizen of the Kingdom*.[6] He makes several helpful points, insofar as he highlights the obvious idea that it is God in Christ who brings the church into existence by the work of the Holy Spirit in the hearts of individuals, using the "powerful seed" of His word in our lives. Whitworth notes that church is regarded by many people not so much as a noun defining a group, so much as a verb in which God, by the action of the Holy Spirit, and in conjunction with the word, brings into existence a body of believers. An interesting idea – church as both noun and verb.[7] Whitworth comments also on Jesus' understanding of the Kingdom: according to the four gospel accounts of the life of Jesus, He rarely spoke about 'the church'. Instead He spoke ceaselessly about the kingdom. The church, then, is an expression of the kingdom. Crucially Whitworth notes that "unless it is conformed to the pattern of the kingdom, it will lack any authenticity". It is the authenticity of the rebel church that is a key sub-text of this book. The kingdom of God is not the same as the church. The kingdom creates the church. The church should bear witness to the kingdom.

And what is the Kingdom?

The Kingdom, then, is the sovereign rule of God, initiated by the earthly ministry of Jesus the Messiah. This rule will be consummated when **"the kingdom of the world has become the kingdom of our Lord and of His Messiah,**

---

[5] *Ibid*. pp. 12-13
[6] *Becoming a Citizen of the Kingdom* by Patrick Whitworth (Terra Nova, 2006).
[7] *Ibid*. pp. 20-21.

and he will reign for ever and ever" (Revelation 11:15). Whenever the word 'kingdom' is used in the teaching of Jesus, it is reasonable and useful to replace it with the word 'rule' – because the kingdom of God is found where the rule of God is.

The first three gospels (Matthew, Mark and Luke) show us that the Lord's proclamation of the kingdom was his core message. Matthew summarises the Galilean ministry in these words: " .... **he went about in all Galilee, teaching in their synagogues and preaching the good news of the kingdom, and healing every disease and sickness among the people**" (Matthew 4:23). The sermon on the mount in Matthew chapters 5 through 7 summarises and spells out the righteousness that is necessary before any person can enter the kingdom (Matthew 5:20). The parables in Mark 7 and Matthew 13 illustrate the 'mystery' of the kingdom (Matthew 13:11 and Mark 14:25).

The expression 'kingdom of God' is not used in the Old Testament, but the concept is found frequently within the prophets. God is often referred to as King, both of Israel and of the Hebrew people (Exodus 15:18; Numbers 23:21; Isaiah 43:15) as well as King of all the earth (2 Kings 19:15; Psalm 29:10; also Psalm 47:2; 93:1–2; 96:10 and numerous other places). A distinction is made between the way that God is King over all and the distinctive way that He is King over His own people, Israel, and through the church. This kingship will have a final consummation, something that still has a future outworking, although God's rule is consummated in the lives of individual believers, no less than in faithful communities of believers. So, God's rule is seen in the history of Israel – albeit imperfectly seen, as Israel repeatedly rebelled against God's sovereignty. In the same way, Israel was constantly involved in warfare against its pagan neighbours (where frequent attacks upon Israel seem to have had a demonic root) and was not always victorious. The prophets accordingly looked forward to a future time when God's rule will be fully realised, not only by Israel, but in the wider world. They describe this in terms of a divine visitation: "**For behold the Lord is coming from His dwelling place; he comes down and treads the high places of the earth**" (Micah 1:3). Zechariah prophesied a time of battle when the whole world would gather against Jerusalem, and yet the Lord will fight on her side, His feet standing on the Mount of Olives outside Jerusalem (Zechariah 14:3). In other places, Israel would be visited by "**the Lord Almighty .... with thunder and earthquake and great noise**" against the hordes of all the nations (Isaiah 29:5–7). His final coming ushers in final judgement (Isaiah 26:21) bringing judgement for the Gentiles as well as for Israel (Zechariah 2:10–11; Isaiah 66:18–24).

Jesus' teachings about the kingdom contrast the present world in which we live, with the future consummation. Jesus made a distinction between this age and the age to come. When a rich young ruler asked Jesus what he needed to do in order to gain eternal life (Mark 10:17) Jesus spoke of the difficulty of entering the kingdom of God. In response to this, His disciples asked incredulously "Then who can be saved?" Jesus' answer contrasted the experience of true disciples "in this present age" with "the age to come". In a number of places, then, Jesus taught about the 'now' of the kingdom and the 'then' of the kingdom. (For examples, see Luke 16:8; Mark 4:19; Matthew 5:14; Luke 22:53; Luke 20:34–35). It is solely in the gospel of Matthew that we encounter the expression "**the close of the age**", which will be concluded by the coming of the Son of Man and the judgement of mankind (Matthew 24:3). Then *the righteous* will be separated from *the wicked* (13:49). The same wording is used in Matthew 28:20 where the risen Jesus assures His disciples of His presence with them "**to the very end of the age**". There is both a now/today time aspect to the kingdom, and a future, eschatalogical aspect. So the pure in heart will see God (Matthew 5:8) and the harvest will be gathered into the barn (Matthew 13:30 and 39; Mark 4:29). Jesus will drink wine in the kingdom with His disciples (Luke 22:30) and people will be gathered from all over the world to sit at the table with the Old Testament saints (see Matthew 8:11–12; Luke 13:29). The consummation is likened to a wedding feast (Matthew 22:1–14), and to a banquet (Luke 14:16–24). Each of these pictures shows a restoring of the close relationship between man and God that was lost at the Fall.

In the recorded teaching and ministry of Jesus, we see how he dealt with Satan, who constantly opposed our Lord. So we are shown the clash between the victorious kingdom of God and the opposing kingdom of darkness, the latter having been defeated at the Cross. Paul referred to the devil as 'the god of this age'. Satan's ambition is to hold people in darkness and unbelief, so keeping them under his control (2 Corinthians 4:4). So, when he tempted Jesus in the wilderness, the devil showed the Lord all the nations of the world, offering to give them to Jesus in return for His worship. This shows that, in this world at this time, the devil has a very real, if ultimately limited, power. Through this power he exercises a tragic control over humans. This then influences, and spoils, our experience of the kingdom of God in this life. Satan's reach is described as being like an enemy from whom people need to be saved (Matthew 6:13) and that of a strong man who defends his 'property' (Mark 3:27). The devil can persuade people to undertake monstrous evil – and we merely need to think of Judas' betrayal of the Lord to see what this can do (Luke 22:3). He attacks Jesus' disciples (Luke 22:31) and attempts to battle against God's purposes in this world (Matthew 13:37-39; Matthew 4:14–15). Satan's kingdom is described as such (Matthew 12:26) and his demons are able to take possession of individuals (Matthew 25:41). There is a tragic warning to all in the condition of those who are described as 'sons of the evil one' (Matthew 13:38) whose lives are controlled ultimately by the devil rather than by God. The age to come will witness the destruction of the devil and all he stands for (Matthew 25:41 and cf. Revelation 20:10).

Throughout Jesus' ministry there is repeated teaching that His mission is a fulfilment of Old Testament messianic prophecy. **"The time has come .... the kingdom of God is near. Repent and believe the good news!"** (Mark 1:15). This is from the NIV translation. Perhaps the old AV has it slightly better when it says **"the time is fulfilled and the kingdom of God is at hand"** – so emphasising the fulfilment of prophecy and the reality of God's kingdom in the here and now. John the baptiser used similar words as he prepared the way for the ministry of Jesus: **"Repent, for the kingdom of God is near"** (Matthew 3:2). The Baptist expounded what the reality of kingdom meant: **"He will baptise you with the Holy Spirit and with fire. His winnowing fork is at hand, and he will clear the threshing floor, gathering up his wheat into the barn and burning up the chaff with unquenchable fire."** Plainly the reference to fire is an apocalyptic outworking – it is something yet to happen. Jesus also spoke of fulfilment, revealing that the prophet Isaiah's prophecy was being fulfilled in Him (see Luke 4:18-21).[8]

Let us explore a little more the reality of *the kingdom* and its contrast with *the church* which is supposed to stand as an ambassador for that kingdom. Jesus showed the kingdom in history (i.e. as an historical event) in Himself, as we have already seen. Although kingdom signs were clearly present, the apocalyptic consummation had not yet occurred, and Jewish people generally then (as today) saw the coming of the Messiah as ushering in an apocalypse – a complete change in the world, specifically the rule of God upon the earth. But in the time of Jesus the apocalypse did not happen.

Jesus made it clear that the kingdom was active and

---

[8] If you are prepared to mark your Bible, it is instructive to underline or highlight the number of times the word 'fulfil' is used in the Gospels. e.g. in the NIV it is encountered five times between Matthew 1:22 and Matthew 3:15.

"advancing forcefully". In Matthew 11:2–6, we see what was happening: "**The blind receive sight, the lame walk, those who have leprosy are cured, the deaf hear, the dead are raised, and the good news is preached to the poor.**" So the kingdom was being inaugurated in Jesus' earthly ministry – not as some people may have expected, but perfectly in line with prophecy. Jesus showed that blessings of Messianic salvation were indeed present and visible. This is clear from his reply to John the Baptist (when the latter was imprisoned), part of which is quoted above, and the Lord's other words about what was happening. We can see that apocalyptic consummation was still to come in the future, but signs of the kingdom were *already* present as the blind received sight, the lame walked, lepers were healed, the dead raised and the good news preached. The kingdom was indeed "advancing forcefully". Jesus pronounced a special blessing on those who were not offended by the now-time character of Messianic fulfilment (Matthew 11:6). The fulfilment *was* happening before their eyes there and then (and, we might add, is happening now and today) and the eschatological consummation will happen in the future.

We see very clearly in the Gospel accounts how Jesus, revealing His kingdom authority and power, undid the works of the devil. Amongst the defining acts of Jesus was the frequent exorcism of demons and deliverance of individuals from demonic power. The Pharisees clearly saw this happening, but attributed it to Beelzebub, the prince of demons (Matthew 12:24). In reply to their assertion, Jesus pointed out that if Satan's kingdom was divided against itself then it could not stand. The tragedy of the Pharisees' outlook (and opposition to Jesus) was that they attributed a work of the Holy Spirit (healing by Jesus) to the devil. In effect they were calling good evil, and evil good. Bizarrely, the author of this book once heard a church person with a penchant for religious syncretism attempt to turn Matthew's account on its head and to 'interpret' what the Lord Jesus said in a completely different way: all religions, this person said, lead to God, because if the religions were divided against themselves then they could not stand! A thoroughly convoluted conclusion, which runs the risk of making precisely the same wilful error as the Pharisees – to call good evil and evil (in this case religious evil) good. It was Jesus' affirmation that, **"...if I drive out demons by the Spirit of God, then the kingdom of God has come upon you"** (Matthew 12:28). Here the Greek verb has a precise meaning (to come, to arrive), emphasising that the kingdom of God was indeed *present* as Jesus ministered.

The church is to be the custodian of the kingdom (Matthew 24:14). Jesus said, "I will give you the keys of the kingdom of heaven" (Matthew 16:18–19). The church in this context should not be seen in the light of subsequent history – where all too often the organised church seems to have been thoroughly rebellious and often unholy – but in the light of the Old Testament background and Jesus' own mission. The word 'ecclesia' was often used in the Septuagint[9] for *the assembly of Israel as the people of God.* Jesus called those who entered into the kingdom "sons of the kingdom" (Matthew 13:38) and a "little flock" (Luke 12:32) who will inherit an eschatological kingdom. However, the church is not the kingdom. As stated earlier *the kingdom is the rule of God, and the places in which His rule is experienced as a reality.* The church is the *people of the kingdom* – those who have received the kingdom (Mark 10:15) by repenting toward God, believing in Jesus, being immersed in and filled with Holy Spirit, and so entered into the blessings of God's rule (Matthew 11:11). The church witnesses to the kingdom (Luke 10:9; Matthew 24:14). The church is the instrument of the kingdom in this world.

---

[9] Jewish translation of the Old Testament into Greek

What did the earliest Christians call themselves?

It is helpful as we consider what the church is, and therefore identify progressively where it presently diverges from – or rebels against – the principles of the kingdom, to consider what the earliest believers called themselves, because they rarely called themselves 'Christians'. For our day and for our time, it is becoming increasingly difficult to use that term, as it has become just too broad. So indeed has the term 'church'. The evolution of meanings has progressed to such an extent that, as people of the kingdom, we are forced to adopt a different mindset and possibly to qualify what we mean when we refer to ourselves as Christians. We may need to identify those who are genuinely kingdom seekers – *people who are looking for a relationship with and through Jesus as Lord and as Saviour.* Whilst definitions may be thought of as tedious, it is essential we have a clear view of these things, and perhaps the lack of a clear definition has aided the progressive and increasing rebellion of much of the 'church'.

In the early early church period, in the centuries after the resurrection and ascension of Jesus and the coming of the Holy Spirit at Pentecost, there were of course no denominations. Churches were known primarily by the locations in which the members lived e.g. 'the church at Thyatira' or 'the church at Sardis'. There was no single name for *the movement of Jesus* – the church. Most of the very earliest Christians considered themselves to be simply faithful Jews who had placed their faith in the risen Lord Jesus – they were what in today's parlance we would call 'Messianic Jews'. They were culturally and 'politically' Jewish, but were genuine believers in Jesus and had received the Spirit. We need to keep these Jewish believers very much in mind as we consider the arguments raised throughout this book. It must be said emphatically that *most of the writings of the early church were provided for us by faithful and true Jews*. There was only a tiny nascent Gentile church in the apostolic period and it is certain that only one of the biblical writers was a Gentile (Luke). There is even an element of doubt about him – he may have been a Gentile convert to Judaism who later progressed to become a Messianic Jew.

So, what were these believers called by other people, outsiders to this new faith? As had Jesus, the disciples began to preach and teach – and to win converts – in the name of Jesus. Other Jewish people began to perceive this as a *new movement* (putting that in modern terms). They used at least four names for this new community within a community:

Galileans

As Jesus and the majority of the disciples were from Galilee, it was natural for them to be identified with that province and all followers dubbed accordingly. There may have been in this geographic distinction a suggestion or intimation that the new faith was not as pure as Judean Judaism. Judeans had a high opinion of themselves and of their religious purity. Some scholars have suggested that Luke 22:59 may be a use of 'Galilean' as a title. References in Acts 1:11 and 2:7, by contrast, are simply geographical references. However, the use of the term by the Roman pagan philosopher Epictetus,[10] who was mightily impressed by the willingness of Christians to die for their faith, suggests that the term had in his day spread from Judea as far as Rome.

Followers of the Way

From the earliest, it was clear that Christianity was not an abstract philosophy, but was in every sense a way of life. Even a cursory review of the word 'Way' in the Scriptures, using a concordance, shows a rich history and special understanding of that term amongst Jewish people. The new way of living and of following Jesus' lifestyle was clear and obvious to those among whom the earliest Christians lived. The term 'this Way' or 'the Way' soon became a descriptor

---

[10] The Encyclopedia Britannica has a useful entry for Epictetus (AD50–135).

for the disciples of Jesus, as they became known as *followers of the Way*. So it was that Saul in Acts 9:2 was empowered to go and search for anyone belonging to the Way. It seems likely that Christians also adopted the term widely as a generic description of their identity in Jesus. Luke refers to the Jesus movement as 'the way' in Acts 19:9, 23 and 24:22.

Nazarenes
The Lord was certainly know as Jesus of Nazareth, or Jesus the Nazarene, and so it was natural again that His followers should acquire that title. The term is used in Acts 24:5 where Tertallus accused Paul of being the ringleader of the Nazarene sect. This title was surely not intended as a compliment and it is unclear that disciples of Jesus adopted the term. However it was adopted later by some Messianic Jewish and also Gnostic groups as a descriptor of who they were.

Christians
When the Jesus movement reached Antioch in Syria, the good news was preached to Gentiles as well as Jews. Messianic Judaism was now open to non-Jews. It was the beginning of a process that could be argued to have set up a new religion, no longer principally Jewish, and certainly not Jewish in nature. Whether such a divorce from the Hebraic root was intended by God is explored in chapters 6 and 7. It was the Gentiles of Antioch who invented the new name. As believers talked constantly of Christ, for them to be dubbed 'Christian' as a nickname (or term of contempt) was perhaps inevitable.

Here is an interesting thought, and I will leave readers to contemplate it at their leisure! If you ask Christians what the term Christian means, some 90% will say with confidence "It means to be a follower of Christ." If you then ask them what 'Christ' means, a far smaller percentage will give a confident answer. You might if you are lucky get the answer

– "Well, 'Christ' means 'the anointed one.'"! If you persist and ask them what 'the anointed one' means, then a very high proportion will struggle. The truth of the matter is that the word 'Christ' is an English translation of a Greek word (*Christos*) which in turn is a translation of the Hebrew word *Massiach*, which in turn is rendered in English as 'Messiah'. Wherever the term 'Christ' is found in our Latinised Bibles, it is entirely interchangeable with the word 'Messiah', which is a more correct transliteration of the word *Massiach*. Christians might just as easily have been called 'Messiahns' as 'Christians', in the English language!

In the term 'Christian' some satire may have been intended when non-believers used the name. As an example, the 'Augustinians' were a group who led the public praise and worship of the emperor Nero Augustus. It is possible that the people of Antioch coined a Latinised name out of Messiah entirely as a satirical joke, as a contrast with the Augustinian camp. The term 'Christian' appears only three times in the Bible, in Acts 11:26, Acts 26:28 and 1 Peter 4:16. The reference in 1 Peter encourages believers not to feel ashamed should they suffer due to the name that is applied to them. It was not until the second century that Christians began widely to use the name as a self-descriptor. Whilst the satirical origins may have been resented initially, it is difficult to think of a better descriptor for a follower and disciple of the Lord Jesus.

Having looked at three titles used by others about Christians, we now reflect on what the earliest disciples called themselves. As individuals they first used the title **'disciple'**. It was a term common in the ancient near east for the pupils of a teacher. We find the term in Matthew 10:1; Luke 6:17 and John 6:66. Also in Acts 6:1, 2, 7; 9:36; 11:26. Jesus was followed by people, male and female, young and older, who listened to His teaching of the Scriptures and sought to 'follow' Him by imitating His way of life. The Lord's own command to His disciples was to make other disciples, teaching them to do everything he had commanded and baptising them (Matthew 28:19–20). The second term was '**slave**', used as a synonym for believer, or Christian. In the Old Testament, God was viewed as the King of His people, who were by contrast the King's slaves, since a King could do with them as he pleased. This was an age of despotic rulers, so the concept would be well enough understood as a day-to-day reality in New Testament times. (See Romans 1:1; Galatians 1:10; Philippians 1:1; Colossians 4:12; 2 Timothy 2:24; Titus 1:1; James 1:1; 2 Peter 1:1; Jude 1; Revelation 1:1).

Two other titles as self-descriptors had currency: the '**elect**' or '**called**' is a prominent one. In the Old Testament, God called or elected the Hebrew nation to be His 'chosen people'. The New Testament presents Jesus as the chosen one of God – the Messiah. His disciples then described themselves as the *called*, the *chosen*, the *elect*, pointing to the idea that they are partakers in the Old Testament promises (Romans 16:13; Colossians 3:12; 2 Timothy 2:10; 1 Peter 1:2; 2 John 1:3; Jude 1; Revelation 17:14). The '**righteous**' was another title adopted. Righteous people, who stood pure and pious before God, were a feature of the Old Testament, and several Old Testament texts on this are quoted in the New, hence Habakkuk 2:4 in Romans 1:17; Psalm 14:1 in Romans 3:10; Psalm 34:16 in 1 Peter 3:12. So the idea remained alive and Christians saw themselves as made righteous by Jesus. Jesus, of course, is the only truly righteous person (1 Peter 3:18; 1 John 2:1). But having been made righteous through Jesus, Christians could adopt for themselves the Old Testament epithet of 'the righteous' (Romans 5:19; Galatians 3:11; James 5:6; 1 Peter 4:18; Revelation 22:11).

Lastly, having considered what others called the Christians and what they considered themselves to be as individuals, we consider the group titles under which the earliest believers considered themselves. Three terms were used to describe

Christians as a body: '**church**' or congregation/assembly we have already considered. The '**multitude**' was a term used in a way similar to the 'church', meaning once again the gathered congregation, as well as those grafted-in to the covenant promises of the Old Testament. Acts 4:32; Acts 6:5; Acts 15:12 in the Authorised Version use this term. ('Believers', as in the NIV, is perhaps a less accurate translation). Finally '**flock**' or '**flock of God**' brings out the common Jewish metaphor for Israel found in the apocryphal and pseudepigraphal writings. Importantly, we can see how it accords with the statement of Jesus that He is the good shepherd – and that the good shepherd lays down his life for his sheep (see John 10). The believers are those who know that Jesus laid down His life for them – on the Cross.

In conclusion....

It is to be hoped that readers will have followed the discussion to this point. If there is a *rebel* church then there must be a *true or faithful church* against which it has rebelled. Jesus taught His followers to seek the kingdom, not the church. The church must, at the end of the day, be the community of those who believe in, trust and obey Jesus as Lord and as Saviour, who have received the Spirit and who then follow Jesus faithfully as disciples, as we saw at the beginning of this chapter. The idea of *following* implies a closeness in proximity, and certainly not running ahead, going our own way or developing our own theology in defiance of the clearly revealed Word of God. Nor does it allow for a wide distance, being at arm's length (or further) to the left or to the right. *Following* implies humility and a willingness to accept (and joyfully accept) discipline. Biblically we can say that the true Christian is indwelt by the Lord Jesus (John 14:23) through the Holy Spirit. The Bible also teaches that the Christian believer is *in* Christ. This is in contradistinction to being *in* the realm of sin. (See Romans 6.)

The church is figuratively said to be the *body* of Christ:

- **So we, who are many, are one body in Christ, and individually members one of another** (Romans 12:5).
- **For the equipping of the saints for the work of service, to the building up of the body of Christ** (Ephesians 4:12).

The church is the gathering of the believers who come together to participate in fellowship with one another as they worship God and hear from His Word, the Bible. The church contains people with differing spiritual gifts; as stated in the Introduction we are not called to be monotone carbon copies of each other (1 Corinthians 12:4–30). The purpose of spiritual gifts is: **for the equipping of the saints for the work of service, to the building up of the body of Christ, until we all attain to the unity of the faith, and of the knowledge of the Son of God, to a mature man, to the measure of the stature which belongs to the fullness of Christ** (Ephesians 4:12–13).

The church (or body, assembly, elect, called) was founded by Jesus – not as an institution of power structures, but as representatives of His kingdom. Jesus is its Head and its Saviour (Colossians 1:18; Ephesians 5:23). As a person *called*, the individual believer is subject to the Lordship of Jesus (Ephesians 5:24). It must be interesting and noteworthy that, in a post-modern age where wives will often not consider themselves as subject to their husbands (Ephesians 5:23), we seem to have wide parts of what styles itself as 'church' that does not consider itself subject to its Lord! The Bible does not provide a detailed blueprint for church government. It does, however, tell us that there are to be elders, who govern in the church. These elders are to be appointed by the laying on of hands (1 Timothy 4:14; 2 Timothy 1:6), which suggests that people cannot appoint themselves as leaders and are always to see themselves as subject to authority. Elders are to teach sound doctrine and refute error (Titus 1:9; 1 Timothy 3:2). The need for an apostolic laying-on-of-hands, where the hand-laying is seen as a contiguous succession from the time of the apostles, is not clearly taught in the Bible. It is an assumption held by some. Indeed this might be thought a conceit of some parts of the church, designed solely to provide for their leaderships what might be thought of as a 'lock' on what they consider to be 'apostolic succession'. The position, then, of individual believers who find themselves under the authority of church leaders who may quite obviously and clearly *not* hold to the basic tenets of the faith, is not scripturally clear. In these cases, perhaps, the laying-on-of-hands may need to be undertaken by those whom the believers themselves recognise (and have tested) as being faithful and trustworthy believers and teachers. Finally the position of 'laity' *vis-à-vis* 'clergy' as adopted in practice by many churches seems to be ultimately unscriptural, as we shall explore later.

"Happy are those who have been invited to the wedding feast of the Lamb"

Chapter Two

READY OR NOT, HE IS COMING

Certainties and uncertainties

The purpose of this chapter is straightforward: it is to help set the scene as regards the visible return of Jesus in glory, something that Jesus Himself often spoke about. Why is this necessary or indeed important in this book about the rebel church? Many who are already believers in Jesus will have well-developed ideas about this subject, whereas church-goers who do not consider the Bible to be authoritative, will probably consider that this is a subject which is (at best) of only secondary importance, and one that is only elevated and promoted by 'evangelicals' who, they say, seem to be fixated on the subject. As the Lord, however, spoke frequently about His return, it would seem to be rather dull-witted at best, and sheer folly at worst, to ignore a matter which is, irrespective of your detailed views and prejudices, clearly a rather important one!

The title of this chapter is taken, with permission, from Stephanie Cottam's book *Ready or Not – He is Coming*, which, despite its title, is not a book primarily about the Lord's return in glory. In fact it is a book that examines the relationship of Jesus, as Bridegroom, to His church – the Bride. Stephanie Cottam seeks to explore the following questions:

• How long did a first century Jewish bride wait for her groom to take her to his home?

• How long must we wait for Jesus to come to claim His Bride?

• Is the modern church becoming bored with the wait?

• What was the significance of the betrothal cup to groom and bride, and how does this link to the communion cup from which Jesus invites us to drink as we think of him?

• What did it mean to decline a wedding invitation in Jesus' day – and do individual believers risk declining their Lord's wedding invitation today?

Cottam challenges all believers to acquire a sense of the sheer honour that attaches to our personal invitation to the wedding feast of the Lamb. (Alert readers of this book will have spotted that the end of each chapter of this book declares, in the words of Revelation 19:9, that the one who is invited to *the* wedding feast is 'happy' (in the words of the Good News Version of the Bible) or 'blessed' (in the words of the NIV and AV translations). Both words give a sense of the sheer amazement at being so invited, and the joy of responding). By looking at the first century Jewish wedding customs that would have been so familiar to Jesus, Stephanie Cottam brings alive some important eschatological truths. For the purposes of this book, we can affirm at least this: Jesus has stated that He will return and that not all His church will be ready (or pleased?) to see Him. Are *you* ready?

In setting the scene on the return of Jesus, we must once again pursue the subject as best we can directly through the pages of Scripture. Whilst we do not want this book to be perceived as too academic, it seems best and most honest to review it in this way. At least then we will have a sense of the biblical authority we have for making these claims. We will not be too dogmatic about the detail on this. It is a fact that there are several main and competing (and mutually exclusive) theories about what the biblical data is telling us. What is recorded here is what might be described as a normative biblical view, but we readily recognise there are other views that are sincerely and seriously held. It may be that, at the end of the day, the lowest common denominator, and the one thing upon which all normative Christians are agreed, is that the Lord Jesus *will* return!

Whilst it is important to see the second coming in its broader context, readers are invited first and foremost to perceive the status of the church at this future time, the status of the church identified in the New Testament, and to ask themselves: is this primarily a *faithful* church, or is it a *rebel* church? The next several sections of our book are borrowed, with permission, from Glory to Glory Publications' useful book *The Bible Student*. Readers will notice, then, a slight change in style and tempo as we switch from written discourse to a straightforward Bible study:

What do we mean by the Second Coming? This means the visible return of Jesus, the Messiah, to this world; a still future event. Note that as this study deals primarily with the future, we approach it with a sense of caution and humility. We need to recognise that although the fact of Jesus' return is certain, it is unwise to be too dogmatic about details. Greek words used in the Bible in reference to the Messiah's return are 'Parousia', 'Aposcaupsis', 'epithaneia', and others. **All imply a visible return.**

How do we know that there will be a visible return of Jesus to His World?
The Old Testament clearly predicted the first coming of the Messiah, even giving details of his death (see especially Isaiah 52 and 53). Yet the majority of the Hebrew nation was unprepared and blind to the things that were happening when Jesus began His ministry in Judaea and Galilee. The Bible is equally emphatic about Jesus' visible return – the second coming. Jesus Himself referred to His second coming more than 20 times and there are more than 200

such references elsewhere in the New Testament. As Jesus fulfilled all the prophecies concerning the coming of the Messiah contained in the Old Testament, so will He fulfil prophesies relating to His second coming. See especially Acts 1:11 and 1 Thessalonians 4:14. See also:

Psalm 22:1, 7, 13–18
Acts 1:11
Matthew 24:21–30
John 14:3
Romans 11:25–26
1 Corinthians 1:7
Philippians 3:20–21
1 Thessalonians 1:9–10; 2:19; 3:12–13; 4:16, 18
Titus 2:13
Hebrews 9:28

Before Jesus' return, certain things will already have happened....

A long time will pass after the first coming. Time is relative and is not a 'problem' for God, but it is a problem for humans!
Matthew 24:6–8, 48; Matthew 25:5, 19
Note that the scriptures emphasise the absolute necessity to be prepared for Christ's return at any time – and of course He may return for any one of us as individuals at any moment!

The Hebrew people will be preserved as a nation in dispersion. At the time of the end, they will return to the land that God promised to them. Whilst controversial, many hold the view that this is happening.
Deuteronomy 30:3
Isaiah 11:10–12
Isaiah 60:9
Jeremiah 30:11, 18; 31:10–13
Ezekiel 36:24–36; 37:1–11

Luke 21:24 (Many today consider that the time of the Gentiles has now ended.)

Romans 11:25 (There will be an increasing turning among Jewish people to their Lord – Yeshua [the actual Hebrew name for 'Jesus'].)

The gospel of Jesus must have been proclaimed across the entire world. This again has now virtually happened. Although not completely fulfilled, this emphasises the urgency of missionary work.

Mark 16:15; Matthew 24:14

Many false religions will arise – some in the name of Jesus.

Religions will be marked out by their refusal to acknowledge the deity of Jesus, the truth of His propitiatory death on the cross, or the truth of His resurrection from death. Some sects and religions (e.g. the Russelites, Christadelphians, Christian Scientists, Mormons etc) will claim alignment with what might be called normative Christianity. We noted in the Introduction to this book that the very term 'Christian' is now inadequate to truly define who are the disciples of Jesus. There will be a new emphasis on aligning the religions and preaching that ultimately they are all one, under 'god'. This is a heresy, but will be encountered more and more in the future.

Matthew 24:5, 11, 24

Luke 17:23

2 Peter 2:1–2

2 Thessalonians 2:3

The times of the Gentiles must have run its course – Gentile domination of Jerusalem and the ancient lands of Israel will end – Luke 21:24.

Jesus described the approach of His return as being like birth pangs. The pangs arise so we know that something is about to happen. Jesus' explanation of the future is contained in Matthew chapter 24. Readers may want to pause and read that chapter in its entirety.

At the time of Jesus' return, certain things will still be happening...

Unprecedented calamities – earthquakes and associated societal dislocations, political crises, godlessness, persecution of the true followers of Jesus, whether they are Jewish or Gentile. These will be unprecedented in the sense that their intensity will increase, there will be more of them, and they will happen together.

Daniel 12:9–10

Joel 2:31

Zephaniah 1:14–18

Matthew 24:9–10, 21

Luke 21:11, 25

2 Timothy 3:1–5

Organised Christianity will be absorbed into 'the world'. There will be global apostasy – a turning away from Christ to other things. Christian 'religion' will in different ways become cold, formal, asleep, or aligned to other religions. Sadly, the so-called 'church' will be as unprepared for the Second Coming as the Hebrew religious leaders were for the first coming. In both cases the religious leaders should have been alert and aware. In the past they were not. In the future (present?) they apparently are not.

Matthew 24:3–4, 9, 12, 24, 44; 25:1–13

Luke 17:26–27, 30; 18:8; 21:34–35

Mark 13:36

1 Thessalonians 5:1–6

2 Peter 3:3–4

Revelation 3:15–18

There will be a worldwide fear for the future.
Luke 21:25–26
Some believers will be expecting His return. There will be a hidden remnant that will be ready, waiting and scattered across the world, from all races.
Daniel 12:9–10; Matthew 25:1–3, 8; Luke 21:35–36

There will have been a return of Jewish people to Israel on a large scale.
Isaiah 11:11–12; Ezekiel 37:11, 14, 21–22

A global dictator and religious leader will appear. It appears he will arise in Europe, but, once again, we should not be dogmatic about this. He will gain worldwide power. He will be religiously followed – and feared. After being victorious he will have designs upon Israel. This leader may be aligned with, or may be identical to, the apostate leader of a reunited "Christendom" – The Antichrist. This person may be the ultimate architect of harmonized religion, or out of the world religions he may form a new, final religion.
Daniel 7:8 (the 'little horn' is the Antichrist); 11:36–45; 12:1
Matthew 24:14–16; 2 Thessalonians 2:3–12
Revelation 13:3–18; 19:17–20

Once again we emphasise in relation to the immediate preceding section that it is unprofitable to be too dogmatic about the details, but the general outline is plain to see. There will be a global politico-religious leader/ship that is in opposition to Christ – and ultimately this will be destroyed by Christ.

The world will be in the throes of a final great war. A war ultimately against God, involving the Jewish people in some way, and centred on the land of Israel. This is called Armageddon. Israel will be seen as defenceless. Many Jewish people will turn to Jesus (Yeshua) as their Messiah,

because of the great distress at that time. But the Lord will have the final word in this. The enemy will not prevail.
Ezekiel 38:8–12, 15, 21–22
Joel 3:1–2, 9–11, 14
Zechariah 12:1–10; 14:1–9
Romans 11:26–27
Revelation 16:14, 16

Note: Some argue that elements of these prophecies have already passed. Overall this seems not to be the case. But some prophecies certainly did have both a short-term or near-term outworking, and a second longer-term outworking. Some of the prophecies referred to in this study will be in this short-long term category. The short term outworking would have been in biblical times, but the future outworking is still awaited.

The actual coming of the Lord

There are a number of interpretations of what the Bible says. Again we would caution against being overly or divisively dogmatic about this. What we can say is that the return will be visible, dramatic and definitive. It will be a surprise to the world at large – and to many in the church, it seems. As Jesus said (Matthew 24:43), and as the apostle Paul wrote, to most it will come like a thief in the night (1 Thessalonians 5:2–4). No one expects a thief, or they would be ready for him! The purpose of the second coming is to glorify the Lord – and His true church, His bride – His 'called-out' from all nations, races and tongues – now at last triumphant. The precise details are somewhat mysterious but most Bible-believing Christians would generally recognize the following:

* Jesus/Yeshua's disciples will be called in some visible, separate way
1 Corinthians 15:51–53
1 Thessalonians 4:13–17
Luke 17:24, 34–36

* The Lord's physical return is clear
1 Thessalonians 3:13
Zechariah 14:4–5

The Second Coming
Matthew 24:27–31, 39; 25:6, 13, 31–23
Luke 12:39–40; 21:27–28, 34–35
Acts 1:7, 10–11
Colossians 3:4
1 Peter 5:4
1 John 2:28

A period of Christ's rule on earth
Revelation 20:1–4
Isaiah 11:6–9
Jeremiah 23:5–6
Zechariah 14:9

The end...
The destruction of evil, the judgment, and the end of the present earth
Revelation 20:7–10; 20:11–14
Hebrews 1:10–12
2 Peter 3:10–13

A New Heaven and a New Earth
Revelation 21:1, 4; 1 Corinthians 15:24–28
Final prayer – Revelation 22:20

The above has been a 'fast and furious' review of the biblical account of the circumstances of the Lord's return. For the purposes of this book, however, we focus primarily on the church's unreadiness for the return, and upon the active apostasy which is prefigured. The 'big picture' above is really the background to the subsequent discussions and challenges in this book. Readers may want to (and probably should!) pause at this point and review the sub-sections and passages above, rather than taking this author's word for it! As you review this material, hopefully, like your author, you will see the consistency of the message and the consistency of the warnings that are being given.

We repeat what was said earlier. Stephanie Cottam's book *Ready or Not – He is Coming* is not primarily about the Second Coming. Nevertheless she does comment upon it. We close this chapter with a perceptive comment from her book:[1]

If you look around you today, you will see there are many of the signs Jesus spoke about, which seem as though they are becoming more and more visible. There are wars. There are rumours, or threats of wars, as one nation rises against another. There are famines across whole countries. We've seen increases of "pestilences" or fatal, incurable diseases. And there has been what feels like an awakening of the earth, as shown by the increase of earthquakes – in intensity, as well as in quantity. Christians around the world are being persecuted for their belief in Jesus as Lord, even in the 21st century, within the UK. You only have to tune in to some television debates or read the news to hear of Christians being sued because they chose to stand by their beliefs, or people being fired from work because of their faith in God, and because "everybody is doing what is right in their own eyes" (Judges 21:25) as the rights of some minority groups in society become worth more than the traditional values of the Word of God, and because, quite frankly, "lawlessness abounds".

"Happy are those who have been invited to the wedding feast of the Lamb"

[1] *Ready or Not – He is Coming*, Stephanie Cottam (Glory to Glory Publications 2012), p. 59

Chapter Three

THE WAY

Tea with Miss Marple

A few years ago your author enjoyed a cup of tea with Miss Marple. Some explanation is necessary, so let me provide it! For those who do not know, Miss Jane Marple was one of mystery writer Agatha Christie's two[1] world famous fictional sleuths, those private detectives who solved baffling cases which always left the police services truly stumped. Both characters, Marple and Poirot, have spawned numerous television series and feature films and their stories are some of the bestselling fiction of all time. Miss Marple was created by Agatha Christie as a white haired septugenarian spinster who lived in an imaginary country village, and who seemed forever to be adjacent to some incipient murder. Allowing that she was a fictional character, how did I manage to have tea with her?

As someone who had recently become involved with 'local preaching' in my church ('lay preaching' in Church of England terms) I was invited to a day's training with fully accredited local preachers. A slight complexity, as someone who was not a formal member of the denomination in which I was then involved, I could not be formally recognised as a local preacher, but was seen as someone who was willing, and with (apparently) a modicum of gifting and a genuine love of Jesus. So it was felt that I would benefit from some training and from meeting the other 'recognised'

---

[1] The other sleuth was of course Hercule Poirot.

local preachers, before I was unleashed upon unsuspecting congregations. I confess I felt a little diffident about meeting with such 'worthies' – as an 'outsider' would I be up to the mark in terms of biblical knowledge and 'soundness of speech'? It was at the training session that I met a charming little septugenarian lady with snowy white hair who was celebrating (if memory serves me correctly) some thirty years of local preaching within her denomination. One could not help but mark the similarity to the fictional Miss Marple. We sat down to a cup of tea on arrival at the training venue and Miss Marple joined myself and several male local preachers at our table. We engaged in the inevitable small talk and then moved on to slightly more serious matters (preaching!) when Miss Marple made a statement that has stuck with me ever since, although I genuinely cannot remember the precise context. Somehow we had got on to the subject of life's struggles and the reality of spiritual opposition and Miss Marple, with a smiling face and an assured tone said, "Ah! but that would require us to believe in the devil, and none of us believe in all of that, do we?" Now, as the Bible tells us that Jesus encountered the devil as a real and personal enemy, and as the Lord Jesus Himself gave specific teaching on the devil, it is a not unreasonable position for normative Christians to adopt when they say that the devil (Satan) is an enemy that we are supposed to take seriously. It is hard to do that if you do not actually believe that he exists!

I repeat, I was an outsider at this local preacher's training event. On behalf of my host who had invited me and vouched for me, I was certainly anxious not to get involved in anything controversial! And when charming Miss Marple made a statement in which she was obviously perfectly sincere, it would have seemed to be ungentlemanly in the extreme to 'take her to task' for it, or to argue with her. After she made her surprising statement, there was a momentary pause whilst several men took stock of the situation. I took several large sips from my tea assuming that one of the gathered 'veterans' might say something wise and thoughtful. No-one spoke. My eyes flitted across the faces of the men at table and everyone seemed to be slightly embarrassed. Still nothing was said by anyone. And so Miss Marple continued her discourse – the rest of which was eminently forgettable, as was the rest of the training day! I suspect that I was not the only person who heard Miss Marple's comment who was surprised, although it is well enough known that not a few within the Western church see references to Satan as being purely 'symbolic' or 'spiritual' and not something that is meant to be understood in a literal sense.

I was slightly saddened on that training day, some ten years or more past. How many sermons had Miss Marple given over thirty years, and what was their content? Whilst it is not unexpected that there might be some variability in understanding, nevertheless when a subject is spoken about as plainly as is the devil and his power structures, are we then free to 'doubt'? Is it to take a liberty – and a very large liberty – for a preacher to cast doubt upon what the Bible affirms – and indeed what our Lord Jesus affirmed? I could hardly have been shocked. This was a good ten years after the Bishop of Durham in the UK had stunned even the media by telling them that he did not believe in the virgin conception of Jesus, nor did he believe in the resurrection of Jesus from the dead. In other words as a senior prelate he did not believe in the core tenets of the Christian faith. If a senior executive in a private company was to tell the world that he did not believe in his company's core products, he would be dealt with swiftly. But the organised church considers it to be 'un-Christian' to deal with rebellion even in its senior ranks.

How is it then that there can be such a divergence in understanding and 'belief' within a church? Does the Lord Jesus provide latitude for such divergence and such disbelief? Part of the answer – but certainly not the whole answer – lies in the way in which the Bible is read and understood. Let me elucidate and introduce you, if you are not already familiar, with three technical terms: hermeneutic, exegesis and eisegesis. But please do not worry! This is not as fearfully complex as these technical terms may suggest! First, *hermeneutic*. This is simply the recognition that documents and texts can be considered in depth prior to being understood or 'interpreted'. So *hermeneutics* is the method of interpretation, especially of Scripture. It is also that branch of theology which deals with the principles and methodology of exegesis. Hermeneutics is merely a technical term – every reader has their own hermeneutic, their own way of reading the Scriptures. Everyone has a hermeneutic, a method of understanding Scripture, whether at one pole it is simply to accept all Scripture as entirely literal, or at the other pole to say that little if anything is literal and instead it is all 'spiritual' (whatever that may mean!). A hermeneutic, then, is a method of study.

Now we come on to the much more interesting – and controversial – bit! This is an area where, frankly, anyone who thinks of themselves as a 'Christian' absolutely must have an opinion and an approach. And indeed they must have their own personal hermeneutic – their own way of understanding Scripture. The two terms are *exegesis* and *eisegesis* which tend to be presented by their respective adherents as poles apart. By and large this is correct – they do tend to be poles apart – although this writer would suggest they do not have to be in practice.

Exegesis and eisegesis are two conflicting approaches in Bible study. *Exegesis is the exposition or explanation of a text generally based on careful and objective analysis.* The word 'exegesis' literally means 'to lead out of'. From the word it we get our modern English word 'exit' – and it is the same root as the name of the Biblical book Exodus, which gives us the account of how the children of Israel were *led out of* slavery in Egypt. In exegesis (or using exegetical tools) this means that the interpreter is led to his conclusions by following the text and reading out of the text what is plainly there.

The opposite approach to Scripture is **eisegesis**, which is the interpretation of a passage based on a *subjective, non-analytical reading*. The word 'eisegesis' literally means 'to lead into', which means the interpreter injects his own ideas into the text, potentially making it mean whatever he wants. In terms of our discussion we might say that eisegesis is to 'read into' scripture what we think *might* be there, or what we think *ought* to be there, whilst exegesis is reading out of scripture what is actually there.

As a summary we can say that the hermenutic which uses exegetical tools is most likely to do full justice to the text, and therefore to what God is saying through the text. Eisegesis is all too often a mishandling of Scripture and often leads to misinterpretation. Eisegesis seeks to deal with what it sees as 'the difficult bits' of Scripture by denying them, and saying they are to be 'read' in different or non-intuitive ways. At its best exegesis is concerned with discovering the true meaning of the text, respecting its grammar, syntax, and setting. Eisegesis, more typically, is concerned with making or 'proving' a point, even at the expense of the plain meaning of words. It is argued, fairly this writer believes, that Scripture itself commands us to use exegetical methods: **Present yourself to God as one approved, a workman who does not need to be ashamed and who correctly handles the word of truth** (2 Timothy 2:15). A diligent student of the Bible will try to be an **exegete**, allowing the text to speak for itself. Eisegesis lends itself to error, as the would-be interpreter generally attempts to align the text with their own preconceived opinions. It is also said, quite fairly, that exegesis allows us to agree with the Bible; eisegesis seeks to force the Bible to agree with us. Here is a simple illustration of the point we are making: in 1 Samuel 18:1 we read that 'David loved Jonathan'. Eisegesis by some 'interpreters' has told us that they were therefore homosexuals in spite of the text nowhere claiming this (and indeed elsewhere in the Bible we know that both men were married and were also fathers). Two points need to be made: firstly, you can make the Bible say anything if you want to, using the 'tool' of eisegesis; and, secondly, it has rightly been said that, 'a verse taken out of context is a pretext.'

Quite how Miss Marple reached her conclusion that as regards the devil we were not to "believe in all that" is open to question. One suspects that the tool of eisegesis was the mechanism, but there may have been an underlying unwillingness to submit to the authority of scripture. As Christians we are called to submit to the Word that God has given to us. The default position for any believer surely is to accept the word of the apostle Paul: **All Scripture is God-breathed and is useful for teaching, rebuking, correcting and training in righteousness** (2 Timothy 3:16).

We will pause our thinking on this subject here. Suffice to say that the way that we approach Scripture will have a fundamental influence on how we live out our Christian lives and what we perceive as being acceptable and unacceptable.

Thus far in this book we have looked at the kingdom of God and the expectation of the return of Jesus Christ as two foundation stones for understanding the nature of the church, and how a rebel church can deviate from the biblical norm. We have suggested that, whether or not the church is ready, one day Christ *will* return as King over all the earth and that the Bible is abundantly clear that not all who purport to be His followers will be ready (or pleased) to see Him. For the remainder of this chapter we seek to reinforce and re-emphasise the 'called-out' nature of the church. We do this by seeing it as "The Way" – one of the terms adopted by early believers to describe themselves.

The People of the Way

One of the earliest terms used to describe Christian believers (Acts 9:2), it seems to have been adopted both by Jewish religious and secular communities, both in a positive and in a negative way. In the Old Testament 'way' was often used as a metaphor to describe human modes of behaviour, and frequently with some ethical evaluation. This would contrast what was seen as *the good way* with *the evil way* (Good – Psalm 1:6, Proverbs 8:20; 12:28. Evil – Psalms 1:6, 119:101, 104, 128). The term "way" was also used to designate the ethical rules set out by God for His people (Genesis 18:19; Exodus 18:20; 32:8; Deuteronomy 8:6; 26:17). This way was contrasted with the ways of men, which inevitably lead into sin (Judges 2:19; Job 22:15; Proverbs 12:15; 16:2).

Whilst the Old Testament uses the term frequently and in different settings, it is in the New Testament that the term finds its fullest expression as the Lord Jesus described Himself as "the way" (John 14:6). What could be more natural than for His followers to see themselves as on a journey, on the way? Here are some early references to the use of this term:

- Saul of Tarsus persecuted those of the Way – Acts 9:2; 22:4.
- Others spoke evil of the Way – Acts 19:9.
- At Ephesus there was a riot about the Way – Acts 19:23.
- Paul confessed to worship God according to the Way – Acts 24:14.
- Felix the governor had gained some accurate knowledge about the Way – Acts 24:22. Paul's use of the term in his defence before Felix suggests that it had at least semi-official acceptance.

So what was the meaning of *the way*? How are we to understand the significance of Jesus' use of the term? We can make two bold statements here:

Jesus taught about two ways – Matthew 7:13–14
- The broad way that leads to destruction
- The narrow way that leads to life

Jesus claimed to be *the* way – John 14:6
- The way to truth and life
- The only way to the Father

The Way of Jesus

Without trying to be completely definitive in this, a number of helpful suggestions have been made about how the term *the Way* would have been understood in the earliest church community. Each seems to have the ring of authenticity about it. *The Way* was:
- The teaching of the gospel
- The Christian's conduct directed and guided by the gospel
- The Christian community in general
- The way of salvation – Acts 16:17
- The true way of God – Acts 18:25–26

As noted, the term was almost certainly an early self-designation of the Jewish Messianic community in which they saw themselves as the 'true way' within their larger Jewish community – Acts 24:14. In addition, the term probably referred to being a disciple of Jesus as to be treading 'the Way' in both doctrine and life. Without, it is hoped, being too repetitive, we can say that there were a number of facets to this new life of following Jesus as 'the Way'.

Following Jesus was:

THE WAY TO GOD...

Jesus is the only way to God – John 14:6; Matthew 11:27. Through Jesus, both Jew and Gentile have direct access to the Father – Ephesians 2:18.

THE WAY TO TRUTH...
Jesus came to this world to bear witness to the truth – John 18:37.
He offers the truth that sets us free from the bondage of sin – John 8:32–36.
The truth that calls us to be renewed in righteousness and holiness – Ephesians 4:20–24.

THE WAY TO LIFE...
Jesus came that we might life more abundantly – John 10:10.
He offers a life with:
Love, that passes knowledge – John 15:10; Ephesians 3:17–19;
Peace, that surpasses understanding – John 14:27; 16:13; Philippians 4:6–7;
Joy, that is inexpressible – John 15:11; 1 Peter 1:8.
He offers life beyond this life – John 11:25; 1 Thessalonians 4:13–18.

THE WAY OF PRAYER...
Jesus taught us how to pray, to pray diligently and humbly – Luke 11:1–13; 18:1–14.
He serves as High Priest, Intercessor, and Advocate as we pray – Hebrews 4:14–16; 7:25; 1 John 2:1.

THE WAY OF SERVICE...
Jesus came to serve, and taught His disciples to do likewise – Matthew 20:25–28; John 13:12–17.
Because of this, His followers are to serve one another in *agape* love – Galatians 5:13; 1 Peter 4:9.

THE WAY OF SUFFERING...
Jesus had to suffer in order to save us – before entering His glory – Luke 24:25–26.
Jesus calls us to follow in His steps – 1 Peter 2:20–23.
Sooner or later, suffering for Jesus the Messiah is likely

to visit us, so we are called to be ready – 1 Peter 3:14–17; 4:1–4, 14–16.

THE WAY TO GLORY...

Jesus will one day be revealed in glory – 2 Thessalonians 1:10.

By grace it has been made possible for those believers who live a life worthy of His call, and accomplish what they are prompted to do by faith, to glorify Jesus and to be *in* Him – 2 Thessalonians 1:11–12; Colossians 3:4.

Your name is Peter...

If it is not to labour the obvious, in a book about the *rebel church*, and in a book written principally for Christians, this may be an appropriate moment at which to ask readers to ponder whether they are on that *narrow way* of which Jesus spoke. There are a number of challenging passages which we do well to consider. Have you accepted Him as your way, the only way, to salvation and eternal life? – Matthew 11:28–30; Mark 16:15–16; Acts 2:38; 22:16; Revelation 2:10. If you have never really considered this, there is no time like the present! Your question then will be: 'Just what does it mean to be a Christian and is it something that I could become?' The first part in answering that question will surprise some. Must I become a Protestant, a Catholic, a Greek Orthodox, or something else? In other words, *which church saves*? The message of Christianity is not to ask Romans or Greeks (for example) to become Protestants. Protestantism has in fact no more power to save than Greek Orthodoxy or Catholicism. No church can 'save' you, but the Lord Jesus can. So what did Jesus say?

Once again, rather than paste-in text from the Bible in answering this, the reader is encouraged to make his or her own private study of what Jesus said, and what the apostles taught. To do this you will need a decent translation of the Bible. The author favours the New International Version or the New King James Version, but there are a good number of helpful translations available in modern language. The author would certainly not rule out use of the older Revised Standard Version or the old King James Authorised Version, but these do use very old-fashioned language and for some that may be a barrier to seeing clearly what God is saying (although the Holy Spirit will help to understand even these older versions – it really depends on the reader's attitude and desire).

We all alike are sinners against God
• See Psalm 53:2–3; Romans 3:23–24
We cannot save ourselves. We need to be saved from the effects and consequences of our sins. We need to be changed through believing in Jesus who died for our transgressions and was raised from the dead for us to be brought into right relationship with God.
• See Romans 4:24–25
God promised from the earliest time to send a Saviour into the world
• See Isaiah 42:1–7; Matthew 1:20–21
God loved the world, giving His only Son for it, that those who go on believing in Him may go on having eternal life rather than perishing.
• See John chapter 3
Jesus said we need to be born again
• See John chapter 3. See 1 Peter 1:23

These are not 'proof texts' to settle the argument. But they should give all readers a sense of what God is saying through Jesus His Son and throughout the witness of Scripture. If readers are serious about relationship with God, then now is the right time to do some genuine searching. You may well have a Christian friend who can help you if you feel out of your depth on this. You may have a church near to where you live that can help you. But, to get any further, you really have

69

to begin to see your need, your own rebelliousness against God, who sent His Son to stand in your place and receive the punishment that actually should be yours. But the final decision is in your hands. Will you accept or reject Jesus?

Many will genuinely have a sense that there is something missing in their lives and would like to find out once and for all what that 'something' is. Yet those who find, discover not a thing but a person.

Here is an interesting thought: your name is Peter, whether you are a male or a female. That requires some explanation so let's dig a little deeper into it! There is one question that absolutely everyone in this world has to answer, sooner or later. We may ignore the question and so refuse to answer it directly, though even by ignoring it we are making our answer, albeit a negative one! In the New Testament, some time shortly after the miracle that we call 'the feeding of the five thousand', Jesus asked a question concerning what the people were saying about who He is – which then led to a more personal question. We pick up the account in Luke 9:18 [but it is repeated in Matthew 16:13–19 and in Mark 8:27–29].

One day when Jesus was praying alone, the disciples came to him. "Who do the crowds say I am?" he asked them.

"Some say that you are John the Baptist," they answered. "Others say that you are Elijah, while others say that one of the prophets of long ago has come back to life."

"What about you?" he asked them. "Who do you say I am?"

Peter answered, "You are God's Messiah."

Luke 9:18–20, GNB

This was the Peter question. It was no idle question. Jesus was teaching His disciples what they needed to confront, namely His identity. They all knew that God was going to send a Messiah (or 'Christ' to use the English from Greek translation). God's *Messiah* or God's *Saviour* was anticipated in first century Judea and Galilee (the two provinces where the Lord did all His teaching), with a real sense of this being imminent. The question was at the back of everyone's mind: could Jesus be the Messiah? "**What about you. Who do you say that I am**?" We get a sense of the disciples' reluctance to respond. Who would have the courage to say that Jesus was God's long awaited anointed one – the Messiah? Probably you could have heard a pin drop once Jesus asked the question. There would have been a pause as the disciples looked at each other. It was an electrifying moment. It was bold, and it was the (often headstrong) Peter who broke the silence. Although he could not really understand the full implications of what he was saying, Peter got the answer right. And now we turn to you, dear reader. You are thinking of your (other) name as being 'Peter', and there is no getting away from it! Like Peter in the Bible, it is *you* who have to answer this question! *Who do you say that Jesus is?* Your relationship with Him through eternity will be settled by your answer. It is a serious question that requires a serious answer.

"Happy are those who have been invited to the wedding feast of the Lamb"

Chapter Four

ITCHING EARS

A key text....
What have we established so far in this book? Plainly there are some real and problematic issues around *what* is believed by many who call themselves 'Christians', not least their leaders – those whom the Lord Jesus referred to as 'shepherds', and those who, ideally, should be fulfilling the duties of pastors, teachers and overseers in the body of believers (also known as brothers, Christians, those on the Way) as depicted in the epistles. We have refreshed our minds on what constitutes the church from a biblical perspective, and how this differs from the kingdom of God (essentially, where the rule of the King is operative). We have seen that where there are problems, they are problems with the church, not with the kingdom. The fact that Jesus will return for His church has been explored, especially in the light of the fact that Jesus was clear and explicit that not all His church will be ready or willing for His future reign in glory. And we have looked at the foundational element of precisely how people choose to read and understand Scripture, suggesting that it is in our choice of personal method (hermeneutic) for understanding Scripture that we are likely to encounter the risk of getting things badly wrong. Indeed, it might be asked, if we harbour a rebel heart (i.e. an unwillingness to submit to the authority of Jesus as *Lord*) whether our hermeneutic may have been selected so as to reinforce our preference for rebellion. To repeat what was stated in the

Introduction to this book, the way most serious Christians read the Bible is to take the text at its plainest and simplest meaning – in other words, how the writer clearly meant the words to be read and understood. We should only read the text in another way if it is quite obvious that the writer or the context demands that it be read differently. That is the approach adopted in this book.

If there is a single key text for this exploration then it is probably this: "...**the time will come when men will not put up with sound doctrine. Instead, to suit their own desires, they will gather around them a great number of teachers to say what their itching ears want to hear**" (2 Timothy 4:3). It would be all too easy to characterise the debate explored within this book as one between so-called 'liberals' and so-called 'conservatives' within the church. It would, however, be interesting to hear an avowedly 'liberal' cleric or theologian explain away this text. Shortly we will examine the context in which Paul wrote this warning to Timothy, but 2 Timothy 4:3 is in all respects a stand-alone verse. It is difficult to avoid the conclusion that, in modern terms, it is the 'liberals' who are being addressed – those who appear to be aligning themselves with the world's agenda and presenting what they call a 'social gospel', which seems somehow to encompass all the world's desires and ambitions and yet, strangely, rejects the clear teaching of Scripture on those same questions! There is little doubt that a 'braveheart' liberal theologian will take great delight in expounding their view that the heart of the gospel is a 'gospel of love' that negates the 'troublesome' moral teachings of the Bible, so it is to be doubted that the challenge above will long remain unanswered! But the nub of the warning from Paul was that "a time will come...." That the apostles foresaw church rebellion can hardly be denied – the Bible is replete with warnings but ... **a time is coming** when this rebellion will be open and barefaced in its defiance.

A liberal theologian would probably say that the false

gospel that 'itching ears' want to hear is that of the so-called prosperity theology,[1] where you are seen to place your faith in Jesus and then get rich (quick!). The more you give to God, the more God is seen to owe back to you! This is a slot-machine theology where God is supposed to reward His followers in direct proportion to their financial giving. Most Bible believers would have real sympathy for this disdain for a patently false teaching, but it is hardly likely that this foolishness is what the apostle Paul had in mind as he wrote to Timothy. So what was Paul writing about?

Paul wrote two letters to Timothy. Timothy was a younger Christian leader, son of a Jewish mother and a Greek father. But it was to his mother's faith that he adhered and he became what would be known in modern terms as a Messianic Believer – a Jew who believes in Jesus as Lord and as Messiah. Paul's first letter deals with three main concerns: false teaching infiltrating the church, especially that of the Gnostics,[2] secondly church administration and, thirdly, the character of Christian leaders. Paul's second letter to Timothy consists of personal advice to Timothy and its main theme is endurance – carrying on bravely despite opposition. Timothy is encouraged to go on witnessing faithfully to Jesus as Messiah, and to hold to the true teaching of the good news and of the Old Testament. In 2 Timothy 1:13 Paul reminds Timothy that what he has previously heard from Paul, he should **keep as the pattern of sound teaching, with faith and love in Jesus** the Messiah. Paul recognised the need for sound teaching. Do we recognise that same need today? For **a time is coming**....

Paul encourages Timothy to keep on reminding the believers of 'these things', by which he means *sound* teaching (2 Timothy 2:14). And then in chapter 3 we reach Paul's comment on godlessness in the last days: "**But mark**

[1] Sometimes called the 'prosperity gospel'.

[2] Detailed analysis of Gnostic beliefs is beyond the scope of this book. Interested readers will acquire a fuller account in the author's book *The Empty Promise of Godism* and especially chapters 5 and 6.

this: There will be terrible times in the last days. People will be lovers of themselves, lovers of money, boastful, proud, abusive, disobedient to their parents, ungrateful, unholy, without love, unforgiving, slanderous, without self-control, brutal, not lovers of the good, treacherous, rash, conceited, lovers of pleasure rather than lovers of God" (2 Timothy 3:1–4). We must be honest as we appraise this warning. There have always been times when people, even within the church, have been disobedient in the ways suggested above. When in the past things have looked bad from a Christian perspective, believers have frequently wondered whether indeed they were living in *the last days*; but, says Paul, **a time is coming**.... Whilst in the past terrible things have been done and allowed by that which calls itself church – we think for example of large sections of the church which simply turned a blind-eye to the enormities of the slave trade in the eighteenth and early nineteenth centuries – whilst abuses have been allowed or ignored, it is probably true to say that the church never gloried in these abuses. Instead those churches tried to *hush them up*, to use a modern phrase. But, **a time is coming**.... It seems that a time is coming when the church will indeed glory in rebellion, rejecting sound doctrine, and instead will adopt falsehood and the most blatant disregard of Scriptural commands on righteous living.

Some might argue, on a superficial reading of 2 Timothy 3 that Paul is referring to the world at large, rather than to the church. It would be comforting to think so. Certainly the world at large will become increasingly godless and it is ultimately this godlessness, including persecution of true believers, that will occasion the Lord's return in glory. The whole context of 2 Timothy 3, however, seems to be very much about the attitude and the praxis *of the church* – not the world at large. Indeed we often forget that chapter and verse numberings are not part of the original biblical documents, so there is a seamless connection between 2 Timothy chapters

2 and 3. As 2 Timothy 2:25 is certainly talking about the church, and as 3:4 definitely is, we cannot easily suggest that verses 3:2–3 speak of something different!

What did the Lord Jesus teach about a rebellious church?
As the Lord spoke a great deal about rebellion, both in the generic sense of mankind rebelling against God and in relation to His followers (i.e. Christians) it is necessary that we look at a great many verses in this regard. So many, in fact, that it will not be possible in all cases to explore the context. If you doubt what is being taught here then there are several things you can do to satisfy yourself as to the rightness or wrongness of the argument put forward:

- You can read around the relevant text, to assure yourself that the author here is not ripping the text out of its context in a way that is a straightforward misrepresentation
- You can (and probably should) read each of the three synoptic gospels (Matthew, Mark and Luke) as well as the gospel of John, and read them with an eye to what the Lord Jesus is saying on this whole subject of rebellion
- You can check back in the Old Testament (i.e. the Scriptures with which the Lord Jesus was familiar) again to review how Jesus saw those Scriptures and the way in which He employed them as He signalled what the future church would look like
- you can check what the Lord spoke about the subject of eternal punishment (i.e. hell) and how often Jesus' teachings were directed towards His disciples rather than to the world at large (which again suggests that Jesus foresaw rebellion as affecting those who purport to be His followers, thus necessitating direct warning to them).

Whilst we are about to look at what Jesus said in Matthew, we should perhaps begin with what John the Baptist taught:

John taught repentance as a necessary precursor to salvation. **"Repent, for the kingdom of heaven is near"** (Matthew 3:2). So did Jesus – the message was identical (Matthew 4:17). When John encountered the religious leaders of his day, the interaction can hardly have been comfortable for them! **But when he saw many of the Pharisees and Sadducees coming to where he was baptizing, he said to them: "You brood of vipers! Who warned you to flee from the coming wrath? Produce fruit in keeping with repentance. And do not think you can say to yourselves, 'We have Abraham as our father.' I tell you that out of these stones God can raise up children for Abraham. The axe is already at the root of the trees, and every tree that does not produce good fruit will be cut down and thrown into the fire**. Plainly, John was the forerunner of Jesus and Jesus described him as the greatest prophet (Matthew 11:11). He recognised, as did all the prophets before him, that Israel was not living in accordance with God's holy laws and that accordingly punishment was coming. John's warnings were direct and urgent. Whilst they enjoyed rights as the chosen people of God, the privileges of that chosenness would not be uniquely theirs forever: they should not rely on their kinship to Abraham as a sort of 'get out of gaol free' card – something that automatically guaranteed their salvation. God could raise up sons for Abraham out of the stones scattered about, said John (Matthew 3:9). But God was not going to raise sons from stones. No, God was going to raise sons from every nation and tribe across the world. In the Abrahamic covenant God made it plain that the blessings of Israel would be a blessing to **all peoples on earth** (Genesis 12:2–3). So God was, and is, perfectly able to 'adopt' as sons[3] all who put their faith in Jesus. But the Pharisees and Sadducees (in Jesus' day the religious conservatives and

---

[3] Just to be clear, 'sons' does not refer to gender. Females are included as well. 'Sons' refers to full inheritance rights and hence the blessings accorded to Israel are also 'inherited' by those who place their faith in Jesus.

liberals, respectively) promoted false versions of the truth. John's message was uncompromising: **the axe is already at the root of the trees, and every tree that does not produce good fruit will be cut down and thrown into the fire**. In scriptural terms, what is found unfit for purpose will be dealt with by God – being thrown into the fire implies that all will be consumed, nothing will be left. It will be a total waste, and total loss. This may also refer to the fires of hell. We are bound to reflect, as we consider John's strong words, whether there is an equivalent warning today for those parts of the church that pay lip-service to the Lordship of Jesus, but whose hearts seem to be far from Him.

Of course the rebellious church might consider that it really does not matter what they believe, or even what they teach, so long as they are performing 'good works' for God. They would probably consider such 'good works' as meeting and matching what John meant when he spoke of producing good fruit. Some are inclined to say (again reflecting their adherence to something called a 'social gospel') that the church's task is 'to help poor people' – and consequently the finer points or life and praxis are simply secondary issues – if they matter at all. They would probably consider that in their *ministry of good works* they indeed produce 'love, joy, peace, patience, kindness, goodness, faithfulness, humility and self control' (the spiritual fruits of which the apostle Paul wrote in Galatians chapter 5). No doubt some churches do seem to produce fruit of this type. By compromising with the world and seeking to make the church 'relevant' they are unlikely to suffer opposition. By making friends with the world some limited measure of 'peace' can be achieved. James 4:4, another stand-alone verse, answers this directly: **You adulterous people, don't you know that friendship with the world is hatred towards God? Anyone who chooses to be a friend of the world becomes an enemy of God**. By yielding to the world in the key areas of morality and religious purity, some churches see themselves as achieving such 'relevance' in the eyes of the world. But are they? And what does Jesus say?

What was Jesus' message? As we have seen, it matched John's call to "**Repent, for the kingdom of God is near**" (Matthew 4:17). It seems that few churches these days are keen to echo Jesus' words and call for repentance. Some church leaders seem to think that people can be excused their sins (or peccadilloes) on the grounds of genetic make up. Some speak of a 'selfish gene' which is said to be an 'evolutionary trait', possessors of which are excused their bad behaviour because 'they cannot help it' and are not therefore responsible for their actions and the consequences that flow from those actions. If people, then, are to repent of anything, it is a vague call to repent of being selfish. Whilst being selfish certainly is an un-Christian trait, this seems to water down – to oblivion – the high moral teaching of the Lord. Matthew chapters 5, 6 and 7 constitute what is universally known as *the sermon on the mount*. Needless to say, theologians are wont to argue about these teachings, but most normative Christians would assert that the sermon on the mount does indeed represent the kernel of Jesus' ethical teaching and provides a perfect template of what Kingdom living is all about. Readers unfamiliar with Jesus' teaching might want to pause at this point and read, or re-read, those chapters.

People within the church harbouring a rebel heart might turn to the first verse of Matthew chapter 7 and believe they hold a trump card against criticism. Christians who call for the maintaining of biblical standards within the church and within wider society at large are often portrayed as 'judgemental'. "Ah!" their critics are wont to say: "Judge not that ye be not judged"! (It is fascinating that the old Authorised Version of the wording springs to their minds! Perhaps this is because it is more poetic – or perhaps because they are simply unfamiliar with the newer translations!). When the Lord Jesus delivered His sermon on the mount

He turned the world's values upside down. But this was no 'revolutionary' lecture or harangue – far from it. Jesus did not come to argue against God's law – He came to *fulfil* it (Matthew 5:17). Jesus uncovers and reveals wrong attitudes in relation to murder, adultery, divorce, swearing, revenge and enemies. Far from raising the bar on 'acceptable' behaviour, Jesus lowers it so that no one can slip underneath unnoticed! Entertaining lustful thoughts is the same as committing the act. Entertaining hateful thoughts is the same as committing the murder. Elsewhere, Jesus invited those who were innocent of a sin to 'cast the first stone'. We have to accept His point meekly – absolutely no one is innocent (and in that particular case, it is amazing to see that no potential 'witnesses' of the particular offence thought themselves fit to do so).

When telling us not to judge it seems clear that Jesus had two targets in mind: *first* the teachers of the Law who were poisoning that same Law. They certainly had a huge beam of misunderstanding in their eyes – they may in a sense have 'loved' the Law but not the God who gave it. They loved rules and regulations and would 'strain at gnats' – little things that ordinary people did 'wrong' – but failed to see the phenomenal sin in their own lives – which by comparison was far worse because they were schooled in the Law. They failed to love the people whom the Law was sent to protect. The bad Pharisees[4] were indeed murderers, adulterers and haters – in all of God's righteous Law they failed to perceive and to live the underlying *hesed* or *agape* – that fundamental requirement to love God first and to love others second. This is what some have called, controversially, *the law of love*. It is rightly argued (this author believes) that it is agape (in English 'love') that underpins all that God does – even the awkward and difficult bits of the Old Testament. But any

[4] Not all Pharisees were bad – and it is argued compellingly although not conclusively that Jesus was closer to the Pharisees in terms of theological understanding and their adherence to the Law, than he was to any other group mentioned in the Bible.

'law of love' could never be the 'law' that 'anything goes'! This seems to be the attitude of many who bandy around Mathew 7:1 –'Don't you dare to criticise me, or you might get judged!'

Jesus' *second* target surely was to the temptation in *all of us* (not just the Pharisees) to judge hypocritically. This is something that God simply will not tolerate. This is where we 'judge' others but typically do the same ourselves – in thought as well as in deed. God will apply to us the rules we apply to others. And in a very real sense, we have to thank God for that! He is *righteous* – just, as well as merciful to those who repent and believe. It is interesting today that in our politically correct world many are judging the motives and behaviours of normative Christianity, yet fail to see the anomaly of their own judgements. So the recently defined 'rights' of various minority groups are seen to trump the 'rights' of Christians to debate biblical standards openly and calmly. In the UK the right to discuss morality coolly and openly in a true pluralist democracy is now being progressively removed under so-called 'religious hatred' and 'equalities' legislation. As an example, where Christians state that living together outside marriage is sinful then they are judged (yes judged, by some within the church and by wider society) as intolerant.

So in what ways are Jesus' disciples to exercise judgement? In the New Testament there are two Greek words involved. One word means, essentially: 'judge in order to condemn.' It is straightforward to see the inference in Matthew chapter 7 that we should not engage in judgement to condemn someone – that is God's exclusive role. The other Greek word is the equivalent of the English 'evaluate'. There is a large difference between the two words. In this world we are instructed by Jesus to engage in the process of *evaluation* but not in *condemnation*. Evaluation helps us to understand, in the light of the gospel, so that we approach individuals and their circumstances with humility and determination

– treating people with mercy, grace, and kindness, and yet with resolve.

The text immediately following the 'speck and plank' issue (Matthew 7:6) from the lips of Jesus is, "...**do not give to dogs what is sacred, do not throw your pearls to pigs**". Do Christians agree with Jesus' statement, made just three short verses later? In order not cast pearls, we are surely required to 'judge' who is being referred to! Plainly there are occasions when to share sacred things will cause evil people (and perhaps even ordinary people) to 'turn' and tear us apart. Christians are to exercise godly judgement in these matters. As noted above, today in the UK even to discuss some matters is likely to land a Christian in court. Sadly, the exercise of judgement in these matters is something that Christians will need to do increasingly in the future as society becomes more and more vigorously opposed to Christianity. (And in practice that means more and more vigorously opposed to Christ).

Jesus told us to judge in Matthew 7:15; 10:13 and 10:17. In Matthew 16:3 He tells us to interpret the signs of the times, in 16:11 to be on our guard. In Matthew 18:17 Jesus tells us how the church must judge its own people. Other places where the Lord Jesus tells us to exercise judgement are: Matthew 24:4, 23; Mark 13:23, 37; Luke 9:5; 12:13–15, 57.

Some of these are clearly instructions about being aware of (and to be wary of) the times in which we live. But all involve the exercise of judgement. And judgement *ipso facto* involves judging people, where they are 'at', what their true motives are, and how they will, in all probability, respond to hearing godly counsel. So we revert to the idea that when we judge (as inevitably we must) we must not be hypocritical. In whatever way we judge others, God will certainly judge us. We cannot hide behind Matthew 7:1 as an excuse for moral cowardice or moral laxity. A refusal to 'judge' is in practice a judgement in itself. We think of those who 'sit on the fence' in a moral crisis, such as those who refuse to condemn anti-Semitism. They are, in effect, casting their vote against the Semites (or whoever the vulnerable group is). All those in pre-war Nazi Germany who saw what was happening but kept silent were (morally) casting their vote against the Jews and against protecting the other targeted groups from cruel persecution.

There are numerous other texts around the rights and wrongs of judging, in the epistles of Paul:

Romans 2:1–4; 16:17
1 Corinthians 2:15; 2:28; 3:3–5; 4:4–5; 5:12
Philippians 3:2; 1 Timothy 5:24; Hebrews 2:1
Also, for perspective, non-Pauline references:
James 2:12–13; 3:1; 4:11–12
2 Peter 2:1–22 (highly relevant in the theme of this book!)

In 1 Corinthians 6:2–3 Paul reminds Christians that saints will be involved in judging the world, and we will judge angels – two quite shocking and sobering thoughts for a disciple of Christ! Since in the eternal realm the church (as Bride of Christ) will exercise authority in the name of Christ, it might seem peculiar if we were completely debarred from exercising judgement in this life – and we are, of course, meant to exercise discernment. But the apostle Paul makes it clear that judging what is happening *in the fellowship of believers* is the task at hand (1 Corinthians 5:12). The world at large will ultimately be judged. We simply do not need to do it. But we are to protect the sanctity of the church itself (v. 13).

So when Christians judge, just how are we to do it? We are not to stand with a scowling face, our hands on our hips laying down the law! As far as possible we do not judge the person, but we must try to show that sin – of whatever kind – ultimately brings ruin. We must always be ready to give an answer concerning the faith, and that can mean declaring God's revealed truth from His written Word. In a church context, one-on-one counselling in private is the first (and preferred) method of exercising judgement. In a church context, two or three must be in agreement that there is something wrong and privately counsel the wrongdoer. If this fails, only then is the wider church to be involved. The Lord Jesus Himself spoke directly about this: **"If your brother sins against you, go and tell him his fault, between you and him alone. If he listens to you, you have gained your brother. But if he does not listen, take one or two others along with you, that every charge may be established by the evidence of two or three witnesses. If he refuses to listen to them, tell it to the church. And if he refuses to listen even to the church, let him be to you as a Gentile and a tax collector. Truly, I say to you, whatever you bind on earth shall be bound in heaven, and whatever you loose on earth shall be loosed in heaven. Again I say to you, if two of you agree on earth about anything they ask, it will be done for them by my Father in heaven."** (Matthew 18:15–20, ESV).

It is noteworthy that this sort of church discipline rarely happens – usually some compromise is reached that is ambiguous in terms of biblical standards. Today the most blatant sin (and, it must be said, heresy) is tolerated within churches! It is to be pondered as to whether this provides the most compelling explanation of the church's absolute decline in the Western World. We must note, with humble thanks to God, that His church is burgeoning in many other parts of the world. And it is notable that those burgeoning churches do seem to take a more biblically faithful stance than their Western counterparts on many of the issues that confront the church and the wider world.

What else did Jesus teach about a rebellious church, in the Gospel of Matthew?

We continue with our reflections on Jesus' words in Matthew by taking certain key statements of Jesus where these seem to touch on the idea of rebellious disciples who are unwilling to accept Jesus' discipline. This will be, of necessity, a fast-paced (but it is hoped, not superficial) review. We will achieve this by taking several key verses/portions and then commenting directly upon them. Once again, readers may want to (and probably should) check out the context:

Matthew 5:13

We will explore this verse later in this book, but it is a key challenge of Jesus to His church. The church can lose its essence, after which it becomes useless. Is today's world-compromised church fit for purpose?

Matthew 5:19

The church that teaches mankind to disobey at least some of God's clear commands will not be rewarded. We must wonder which of God's commands some parts of the church are now teaching the world to ignore. Divorce and remarriage springs to mind, but surely there are other commands that are routinely denigrated.

Matthew 7:13–14

Jesus was totally honest: the road to the kingdom is narrow, and the door of entry is small. But today at least some parts of the church try to persuade us that they have invited in the angelic contractors to widen the road (to a motorway?) and to replace the entrance door with a bigger one! The willingness to compromise with all religions (or, perhaps, the so-called great 'Abrahamic religions') springs to mind as an example. But again there are other areas where parts of the church seem anxious to reach accommodations with the world, in their pursuit of 'relevance'.

Matthew 7:21–23

These are perhaps the most chilling words in the entire Bible. That there are 'many' (v. 22) suggests that rebellion amongst supposed Christians is widespread, and always has been. A reader should at this point perhaps prayerfully conduct a self-audit. What type of believer are you? Do you take a *laissez-faire* attitude to Jesus' commands and to the Bible's clear teaching? Is your God a comfortable and accommodating 'God of love' or a consuming fire (Hebrews 12:29)? Pause now, and consider your answer.

Matthew 10:34–39

Being a disciple of Jesus is not a comfortable experience. Does your church try to make it more comfortable by compromise with the world? Does your church teach truth, or a message that itching ears want to hear?

Matthew 12:30–32

Does your church preach faithfully that there is, indeed, an unforgivable sin of blasphemy against the Holy Spirit? It was the Lord Jesus who said it, so we are bound to take His warning seriously. The denigration of the Bible by some parts of the church, including its wilful misinterpretation, does seem to be relevant here. Consider the context. There were those who were denying that Jesus, who was doing amazing works, displaying divine power as he cast out demons and showed the power of God's kingdom rule. ***We are to pay very close attention to the work of God the Holy Spirit, we must never speak against Him and we must warn others.*** This is crucial when you consider the many ways in which the Word reveals the work of the Spirit. The Holy Spirit convicts of sin, righteousness and judgement; He makes Jesus known and glorifies Him; He inspired the Scriptures, He grows the fruit in believers and He blows where He wills, and we need to be 'born' of Him; we must be baptised in the same Spirit, and go on being filled with Him. And there is so much more that we learn about the precious Holy Spirit and His work. Nothing can be more wonderful than simply His presence. No wonder the blasphemy against Him is unforgivable. Those Pharisees who denied that what Jesus was doing was of God, and instead attributed it to the enemy, were given that most severe of warnings.

Once again, we note that denial of the truth of God's written Word leads to something disastrous: it ignores the powerful truth of *what Jesus actually said* as recorded by eyewitnesses. A terrible undermining occurs as, then, the rebel church fails to perceive the seriousness of its own rebellion, let alone mankind's rebellion. That being the case, what is left to save anyone *from* or *to*? What message is left for a rebel church to proclaim to a world which is itself naturally in rebellion against God anyway? When the work of the Holy Spirit in the inspiration of the written Word – and in the other ways revealed there – is denied, just what is left that can be called Christian? The salt that has lost its saltiness is of no use to anyone, and Jesus told us what its destiny will be.

Matthew 15: 14

To understand the relevance of this to our debate, you really need to read Matthew 15:1–20. But the key point about this text is that the Lord Jesus states plainly that there are blind guides who will lead others astray. Jesus was speaking about hypocritical Pharisees whose studious observance of the Law should have provided them with spiritual eyes and crystal clear vision, but instead they were blind to its truth, especially that the Messiah was standing directly before them! (Luke 4:21). So near, and yet so far.... A key sub-text of this book, however uncomfortable it may be, is that within the rebel church there are similarly pharisaical leaders, who teach those who are blind (those who may be genuinely searching) that the teachings of the Bible are not to be taken seriously, but instead are to be 'interpreted' in line with the culture in which we live, and on the basis of new 'insights' that we have supposedly gained, and new social mores. *Jesus' instruction is clear. We are to leave these blind guides – and to separate from them.*

Again this may be deeply troubling and uncomfortable. Some of us will have hard decisions to make in the future as the church we once recognised as home, becomes more and more indistinguishable from the world. But the call of the Bible, the call of Jesus, is to *be separate* (see 2 Corinthians 6:14–18. This speaks of true believers being separate from unbelievers; a pause to look at that passage is highly recommended!) The call of the rebel church in our day seems increasingly to be to yoke together with unbelievers. This is particularly true in terms of syncretism – banding together with other religions. There seem to be few Christian leaders in the UK – certainly in the 'senior ranks' of the various denominations, who have a coherent, biblical message as to how the church is to deal with other religions.

Three days before writing these lines in July 2013, the UK Government's same sex marriage laws took effect. Shortly, churches will be marrying men to men. Will Christians continue to accept 'spiritual oversight' from leaders who engage with the world in this way? Ultimately the choice and the responsibility must be theirs – and theirs alone. But the words of Jesus we have reviewed through the Gospel of Matthew continue to echo in our ears. There really will be no ability to plead that we did not know what He said.

We could continue working through other teachings of the Lord in Matthew, and we would indeed find perfectly consistent witness if we were to work through the entire New Testament, but at this point enough has been said to point to the real issue at stake.

Perhaps readers should now pause and contemplate their own walk with the Lord, and the trajectory of their own church. Whilst the tone of this book is, of necessity, somewhat negative, it must be acknowledged that there are many churches where the truth of the Bible is taught, and many good and faithful pastors, teachers and ministers do their work, persevering, often sacrificially. They should stand firm and rejoice in what the Lord is doing in their situations. But for many individual Christians, sadly, there will come a time when they know that their local under-shepherd, and possibly their local flock, is untrue to Jesus. **"My sheep know my voice,"** said Jesus (John 10:27). If the Holy Spirit is convicting you that your church is going badly wrong, then the only option for you, after prayer, may be to find a new flock, where the Good Shepherd's voice is more clearly audible. (But, first, maybe consider if you might be the 'anyone' as in Revelation 3:20 who can open the church door to Jesus in your fellowship, like that church in Laodicea. If it is simply 'lukewarm', you may be the one whom God will use to raise the temperature!)

Unusually, I will now suggest that readers put down my book and pick up the Bible. Read Mathew chapter 25 in its entirety. Jesus is speaking in three parables about those unready to meet with Him. But, as you read, mark this: *Jesus is speaking to believers*. His words are not for "them" but for us! Matthew 25:44 echoes Matthew 7:22.

As Christians, we simply cannot afford to take these warnings spoken by our Lord Jesus lightly. He is warning us. Is your church a true church, or is it a rebel church? And if the latter, what must your personal responsibility be? Remember it is your responsibility and no one else's – and one day we must all give an account of ourselves to Jesus. (See Romans 14:12).

Please read Matthew chapter 25.

"Happy are those who have been invited to the wedding feast of the Lamb"

Chapter Five

HOW THE CHURCH LOST THE WAY

Syncretism

When writing a book an author normally has some idea as to content and structure of the finished product – a vision if you like – before he or she begins. At this point in the book I had intended to include a chapter on the drift towards syncretism[1] and how this, again, reflects pressures that are causing the church to *lose its saltiness* – its ability to bring the good news of Jesus to a world of desperate need. It quickly became apparent to me, however, that I could not do justice to the subject in a single chapter, and I do not want this subject to over-burden or skew our over-arching theme about a rebel church. I have already explored this topic from a Christian and biblical perspective in ***The Empty Promise of Godism***[2] (Glory to Glory, 2009) and covered it exhaustively in some 370 pages. The trouble is this: if someone with an open mind wants to engage biblically with this subject, then a single chapter is simply not enough. And if someone with a closed mind – with prejudices that entice them towards syncretism – comes to the subject, then one chapter will provide only a superficial overview that will be brushed aside as irrelevant. So instead of a whole chapter, a few paragraphs and a few propositions will have to suffice!

---

[1] Syncretism – the process of melding or mixing one religion with another.
[2] Godism is a term indicating that someone believes in 'god' but also believes in all the religions. Godism is a philosophy rather than a religion.

If God sent various religions that teach opposing beliefs and lead inevitably to conflict between them, then could He be called 'good' or 'holy'?

The belief that there are many paths to truth is ultimately dismissive of God, as is suggested in the logic map in Appendix 1. The author is aware that any particular line on this map can be debated, but has found that even the most ardent syncretists concede, albeit reluctantly, the overall force of the logic map as inescapable: syncretism (or Godism) is ultimately dismissive of God.

The first basic error in the question posed above, of course, is to suppose that non-Christian religions were somehow 'sent' by God! *Man* has devised many religions and philosophical systems, but man-made religion is always produced by sinful men whose own sinfulness is reflected in the idolatry and deception they produce. Fallen man wants to worship something, but the idols he devises (whether physical or abstract) are hateful to the living God who has revealed Himself, revealed His nature, and has provided the only Way of salvation. The very fact that God is perfectly Holy and perfectly good, means that *He* has the right to judge *us*, not the other way round. That there exist 'opposing' beliefs, resisting God's self-revelation, is because He allows mankind limited freedom. It is man's fault, not God's, that man rebels against God, misusing that freedom!

Do all religions contain some truth?

This idea is supposed to sound very open-minded, tolerant, even-handed, non-confrontational, even 'loving' and 'inclusive', and to contribute towards social cohesion. But dig a little, and the deception in such thinking rapidly becomes obvious. A simple observation: this is thoughtless wording, especially if uttered by a professing Christian. Jesus Christ alone is, as he said, ***the Truth***. Not merely an aspect of truth but *the* truth. However, the objects of worship in the world's non-Christian religions ***are not real***

because they are not alive, they are dead. None of the
'religious figures', founders or idols mentioned in those
'world religions' claimed to be the fulfilment of historical
prophecies, or to be divine, and nor were they raised from
the dead. Adherents of other faiths may imagine that by their
religious activities they can gain some favour from their
deities, but since, by definition those deities are dead – not
alive – they have nothing whatsoever to offer except utter
deception.

Will the 'liberal' church in future become increasingly bold, open and blatant in its syncretism?

The Book of Revelation in the Bible seems to point towards
a new world religion emerging. (See Revelation chapter 13).
This new religion will no doubt have nominally 'Christian'
(or ex-Christian) adherents. The advance of syncretism
will become one of the key departure points for concerned
Christians as they perceive what is happening to the church
they once considered as home, and as they listen for the
authentic voice of the Good Shepherd. How do you boil a
live frog? Slowly and from cold water, so it will not jump
out of your pot – it fails to notice the rise in temperature until
it is too late. How do you introduce syncretism into your
churches? Slowly, and always with the assurance that, 'We
are really preserving the uniqueness of Jesus, but we are just
being loving and Christ-like to our religious neighbours.'

If readers are genuinely concerned about the various
religions and a Christian's relationship with them, and indeed
if they are flirting with the ideas of syncretism, and *if* they
want to review this from a biblical Christian perspective,
then they may want to read *The Empty Promise of Godism*
which is freely available in PDF form on the website of
Glory to Glory Publications. It continues to be available as
a paperback book [2013–14] and may indeed be released
via a print-on-demand volume supplier in due course to
facilitate global access.

Beware of Greeks bearing ... philosophy!

What is philosophy? The answer lies partly in the word itself: *philo* = love of; and *sophia* = wisdom. It may at times have reflected a desire or human search for wisdom or knowledge. It is from the Greek word *sophia* that we get our English word 'sophistication'. Most people do not want to be thought of as country bumpkins! We all like to be thought of as sophisticated, even if we do not actually articulate this desire directly. How often in our churches do we encounter people who refuse to believe certain parts of the Bible because 'we know so much more today'? Philosophy often stands as a challenge to the authority of Scripture.

The title of this chapter "How the Church Lost The Way" is taken with permission from the first book in Steve Maltz's useful trilogy[3] that explores how Greek philosophy invaded the early church and how it has infected its thinking, like a virus, ever since. Indeed some of the structure of this chapter is borrowed, with thanks, from Maltz's 2013 article *A Question No One Dares to Ask* which specifically examines Platonism and its influence within Christian thought from the earliest of times. Why do we need to think about dusty ancient Greek philosophers as we consider today's rebel church? Is this really relevant? The answer is, unfortunately, that it is *highly* relevant and probably, if this is not too sweeping a statement, we can assert that Greek philosophy and its attendant Greek mindset, has probably lain at the root of the vast bulk of the issues and problems in church belief and praxis over the past two thousand years. This is a massively generalised statement and readers may now issue the challenge: "Go on Mr Sammons, explain yourself!" I will suggest, in response, that if readers really want to get to grips with this issue, then they should seek out Maltz's

---

[3] *How the Church Lost The Way – and how it can find it again*; *How the Church Lost The Truth – and how it can find it again*; *To Life – rediscovering biblical church* – see the Further Reading section at the end of this book.

trilogy, and work this out for themselves.[4] Maltz is by no means the only modern teacher to examine these things, but he is probably the writer who has done most to popularise and make it accessible at the 'popular theology' level. But we will turn for the moment to another well known writer who held forth on the same subject. Dr Martyn Lloyd-Jones,[5] in his book *What is An Evangelical* (1992),[6] argues that the believer should, in general, 'distrust reason'. Acknowledging that this was a controversial stance, he stated that the evangelical should mistrust reason and particularly *reason in the form of philosophy*. Lloyd-Jones stated that if we take a bird's eye view of the history of the church, the question of philosophy emerges 'very clearly indeed'. He said that every reformation had been a reaction against non-Christian philosophy, and that one of the early examples of this was Tertullian, who had challenged: 'What has Jerusalem to do with Athens? What has the temple to do with the porch and the academy?' So concerned was Tertullian that he had become a Montanist, a group that so incensed the early church that they declared it heretical. Whatever the rights or wrongs of this outcome, Tertullian's challenge was (and still is) a pertinent one.

Lloyd-Jones went on: 'Philosophy has always been the cause of the church going astray, for philosophy means, ultimately, a trusting to human reason and human understanding.' The philosopher, in his endeavour to encompass all truth, desires to explain everything on his terms. The passage of scripture that speaks most clearly into

[4] At the time of writing there is a Bible study course based on the trilogy, so readers might want to make this part of their church's group study.

[5] David Martyn Lloyd-Jones (1899–1981). Welsh Protestant minister, preacher and medical doctor who was influential in the Reformed wing of the UK evangelical church in the 20th century. For almost 30 years he was the minister of Westminster Chapel in London. Strongly opposed to Liberal Christianity, which had become a part of many Christian denominations, he regarded it as aberrant. He disagreed with the 'broad church' approach and encouraged evangelical Christians to consider carefully their denominational affiliations. He believed that true Christian fellowship was possible only amongst those who shared common convictions regarding the nature of the faith.

[6] See the Further Reading section at the end of this book.

this temptation is 1 Corinthians 1:17 through to the end of chapter 4, with special reference to chapter 2. Things were awry in Corinth because they were beginning to elevate human wisdom and human philosophy. Paul's message shows how this is opposed to the preaching of the gospel. Paul says he has become a fool for Christ's sake: **If any one of you thinks he is wise by the standards of this age, he should become a 'fool' so that he may become wise** (1 Corinthians 3:18). Lloyd-Jones comments that a 'fool' in this context means that the Christian does not trust philosophy and human wisdom over the clear revelation of Scripture.

Martin Luther also was aware of the danger of Greek philosophy which he referred to as 'that old witch, Lady reason'. Luther was concerned because this was a key element of his argument against Rome. Lloyd-Jones comments that it remains true today that Roman Catholics claim to submit to the authority of Scripture. 'Let us grant that they do' (says Lloyd-Jones) ... 'what then is the trouble? The trouble is that they have added Aristotelian philosophy to their belief in the Bible, and that ultimately they are interpreting the Bible in terms of Aristotelian philosophy. That is the great characteristic of the *Summa* of Thomas Aquinas, and it was as the result of this that the evangel, the true gospel, had become entirely hidden.'[7] Lloyd-Jones was anxious that he should not be misunderstood on this matter. He based his teaching on 1 Corinthians 2, where Paul says: **We have not received the spirit of the world but the Spirit who is from God, that we may understand what God has freely given us. This is what we speak, *not in words taught us by human wisdom but in words taught by the Spirit*, expressing spiritual truths in spiritual words. The man without the Spirit does not accept the things that come from the Spirit of God, for they are foolishness to him, and he cannot understand them,**

[7] Lloyd-Jones, *ibid*, chapter 2

because they are spiritually discerned (1 Corinthians 2:12–14; author's emphasis). The things that come from the Spirit are foolishness to mankind. These are things which the Spirit alone can enable us to receive and understand. Verse 15 sums this up: **The spiritual man makes judgements about all things, but he himself is not subject to any man's judgement**. Jesus also showed a disdain for the wisdom of the world (and almost certainly He had in mind Greek/Roman philosophy) **"I praise you, Father, Lord of heaven and earth, because you have hidden these things from the wise and learned, and revealed them to little children. Yes, Father, for this was your good pleasure"** (Matthew 11:25–26).

A question no one dares to ask

And here it is:

WHY ARE THERE NO KIDS FOR FATHER TED?

Or ... why are priests meant to be celibate?
Or ... to be more direct, why can't priests marry and have kids?

To understand the second half of this chapter it helps to be British, or at least to know that 'Father Ted' was the fictional character at the centre of a UK television sitcom called – 'Father Ted', about the humorous travails and ambiguous situations encountered by a Roman Catholic parish priest. The answer to our question may well surprise you as it centres around a single idea from just one man, who lived in Greece at a time between the Old Testament and the New Testament. His name was Plato, and we can blame him for all those Catholic marriages that were never to be, to say nothing of those shameful news items in recent years involving priests and other clergymen. In fact there is a great deal that we can blame Plato for, as we shall see!

Plato was the Greek philosopher who, rather than looking at the world that surrounded him, encouraged us to look inwards at our inner lives, at such matters as the mind, body and soul. He came up with a conclusion – *his big idea* – that would have huge influence on Christianity in Europe. Plato believed that we humans are comprised of body and soul and thought that these were totally distinct from each other but were bound together temporarily during a person's lifetime. This is a position termed dualism (but is to be distinguished from certain other philosophies similarly titled – nothing in philosophy is that straightforward!) To Plato, the soul was dominant, superior and immortal, being reborn again and again in different bodies, gaining in knowledge as it does so. This reminds us of the idea of re-incarnation that is taught by Eastern religions. Plato thought that the soul is where we do our thinking, that part of us that is essentially *us*. On the other hand he taught that the body connects through the five senses with the world around us. Unfortunately, Plato cared little for our world, or for our bodies, which, in his view, trap the soul, preventing it from achieving its full potential. So the soul is seen as good and the body as bad. Fix this in your mind, for this was *Plato's big idea*. So what has this got to do with the modern church?

In the Apostolic Palace in the Vatican is a painting by Raphael. It is known as *The School of Athens* and features a group of Greek philosophers. Clearly seen are Plato and his pupil, Aristotle, in conversation. Plato is pointing above to the heavens and Aristotle is pointing down to the earth. The question we have to ask is this: why on earth should Greek philosophers be commemorated in the capital of the Roman Catholic Church? To answer this, we need to go right back to the beginning: the church as we know it today did not just pop up out of nowhere. It is today's snapshot of a continuous historical process that started when the Holy Spirit descended on that small group of believers in Jerusalem just a few weeks after the Resurrection. **When the day of Pentecost came, they were all together in one place. Suddenly a sound like the blowing of a violent wind came from heaven and filled the whole house where they**

were sitting. They saw what seemed to be tongues of fire that separated and came to rest on each of them. All of them were filled with the Holy Spirit and began to speak in other tongues as the Spirit enabled them (Acts 2:1–4).

Let us consider the overriding mission of the Church. Theologians call it the Great Commission: **Then Jesus came to them and said, "All authority in heaven and on earth has been given to me. Therefore go and make disciples of all nations, baptizing them in the name of the Father and of the Son and of the Holy Spirit, and teaching them to obey everything I have commanded you. And surely I am with you always, to the very end of the age"** (Matthew 28:18–20). The task of the church is to gather people of all backgrounds and cultures into its fold, without being influenced or swayed by the ideas of these people, their backgrounds and cultures. As it turned out, being swayed by converts' backgrounds and cultures was going to become a far bigger issue than anyone could possibly have realised at the time.

Now let us briefly travel even further back in time, to the days of Moses and the people of Israel in the desert. God met with Moses on Mount Sinai and gave him the Ten Commandments and a whole raft of teachings to live by, in order to keep the Israelites pure and holy. The Israelites were surrounded by pagan nations, whose lifestyles and beliefs were diametrically opposed to God's holy laws. Moses knew how important it was that God's people should not be polluted by these pagan practices. Sadly, the Israelites were ultimately to fail, being seduced by rival 'gods' and prostituting themselves to alien lifestyles, and they were reprimanded by God as a result. Before any reader in their pride thinks that they would have fared any better, we must realise that we human beings are easily seduced by 'the dark side' – by demonic forces. It is a part of our nature and that is one reason why we need Jesus in our lives! The point we need to note is that the Israelites, despite being given a set of laws to help them to remain pure and untouched by foreign cultures, religions and 'gods', failed to remain pure, thanks to the basic restlessness of the human heart. This brings us neatly back to the church. What chance did the early church have? How could those early Christians, whose job was to *reach out to the entire world*, fail to become polluted in turn by the very people they were trying to reach?

The apostle Paul gave a stark warning about this: **See to it that no one takes you captive through hollow and deceptive philosophy, which depends on human tradition and the basic principles of this world rather than on Christ** (Colossians 2:8). Little did he know that, within a century, the floodgates would be opened and the true, unadulterated biblical faith in Jesus Christ would be thoroughly swamped by the Greek culture and the human traditions of the day. When Christianity spread westwards from Jerusalem to the lands on the eastern side of the Mediterranean, it was the teachings of Plato that were encountered first. The early Christian teachers, the so-called Church Fathers, had to make a stark decision. *Should we ignore these other teachings, or do we engage with them and even learn from them?* THIS WOULD BE THE KEY. CHURCH HISTORY WOULD BALANCE ON THE DECISION THEY MADE. They made a decision to engage with the Greek culture that surrounded them, a culture that was heavily influenced by Plato. After all, these Church Fathers had themselves been philosophers before becoming Christians, so *what harm could it do?* Trained in Greek thought, they saw no danger in constructing a Christian worldview in the light of the teachings of Plato. One of these teachers, Justin Martyr, held the view that Platonists (followers of Plato) would be so energised and challenged by the similarities between their worldview and that of Christianity that they might even consider conversion. It all went downhill from there!

Remember what Plato believed, his *big idea*, that the soul is good and the body is bad; that everything associated with the soul is good and everything associated with the body is bad. This idea now became thoroughly mixed into Christian thinking. The immediate effect of declaring the body bad and soul as good is an obvious one: if the body is bad then *so are things associated with the body*, particularly voluntary processes like sex. Those who followed 'spiritual' careers in the early church were expected to be celibate, a contrary practice that continues in the modern day Catholic Church and which, we are told, has cost the Vatican millions of dollars in compensation claims. We really need to ponder this in terms of what that particular church avowedly stands for, its stated belief and stated praxis, and what really happens. And we need to ponder this in terms of the Platonic philosophy that first energised it. Incidentally, it is from the name 'Plato' that we get the term *platonic love*, i.e. a love that has no physical expression.

Priests and monks were, and still are, required to be celibate. The Catholic view is that celibacy is a 'higher' calling, in the sense of remaining pure until heaven beckons, when you will be united with Christ directly. Anything in this world to do with our physical body was, to the hierarchy of the early church, dirty, unclean, unspiritual, unholy and un-Christian! *None of this is from the Bible. It is all from Plato, our pagan Greek philosopher.* So, to answer our original question, THIS is why there are NO KIDS FOR FATHER TED!

Now that we have focused our attention and acquired an insight into how Greek philosophy infected the early church, we can take this further and start to look at some other issues. First, what is it to be a Christian? Should we have any sort of a *higher* calling? If you are a born again Christian then the Bible tells you that you *are* three things:

– part of the church

As we saw in chapter 1, the Church is *not* a building, despite what we have been told since the 4th Century, when the State church decided that people could only be saved inside this building that we call 'church'. The Greek word in the New Testament that is translated as 'church', *ekklesia*, simply means 'called out ones'. If you are a Christian, you are part of church, you are a 'called out one'. Remember *Plato's big idea*? Out of this simple idea of the soul being good and the body being bad came the idea that anything *spiritual* was good and everything *physical* was bad. And out of this came the idea that there were *two kinds of Christians*:

1. The special 'spiritual' ones they called *the clergy*. These were the priests and the bishops, etc. These were the career Christians, who acted as the go-betweens between us and God.

2. The rest of us, the 'physical' ones, the 'pew fillers', whom they called *the laity*.

None of this is in the Bible.

– a part of a royal priesthood

All real Christian believers are part of the *royal priesthood*, because we all have access to God through Jesus, by the power of the Holy Spirit. Yet many of us act as if this is not true. We still defer to our pastors, teachers, preachers, worship leaders and even Christian celebrities, placing them on proverbial pedestals and conference platforms. We look to them to minister to us and show us Jesus. This is a thoroughly Greek idea and wrong! We do not require such people to 'offer sacrifices' on our behalf, if we are born-again believers we are priests and we can approach Jesus directly. We do not need 'clergy' to do things for us, as we all have access to God, directly through Jesus our Lord.

– a saint

We are not required to worship dead bones or those who have *cast off their mortal coil in glorious triumph*. Dead saints cannot hear your prayers, only God can. We are all saints, even though we may not always act in a very saintly manner!

We are the church and accordingly we are all priests and saints. We *all* have a higher calling. There is no 'sacred and secular' division, because all believers have a sacred calling.

Greek thinking tells us that the missionary who travels overseas to work in a pagan village, showing God's love to those who have not encountered it, is to be especially revered. We should in no way demean the sacrifice these good people have made, and the hardships they undoubtedly endure. But is their calling *really* any different to those of us with a standard nine-to-five job in an office, or who are students, or working in a thoroughly (and often aggressively) non-Christian environment, where any attempt at communicating your faith would be met with hostility, exclusion and even lawsuits? Who has the higher calling? Neither, because wherever we are in the world we are called to be witnesses – we are called to be missionaries. God commands each one of us to be *in the world but not of the world.* We are to be salt and light in our witness to the world, without being sucked into its ways. Of course this is not easy and it seems to be getting harder all the time! James reminds us of the consequences: **Don't you know that friendship with the world is hatred toward God? Anyone who chooses to be a friend of the world becomes an enemy of God** (James 4:4).

With the simple idea from Plato that the 'spiritual' should be preferred over the 'physical', we get the whole concept of division. We have already heard about the *clergy* and the *laity*, but what about the *natural* and the *supernatural*, the *holy* and the *profane*, or the *sacred* and the *secular*? We all think in this way – we just cannot help it. If we are completely honest, we even divide up our lives into the 'spiritual' part, when we are at church or home group for a few hours a week, and then the rest of the week which we see as *ours*, to do with as we please! How many people, when they leave the church door, head for the pub or the cinema and make that switch *from sacred to secular?*

One word of warning on that last one – God is 24/7, even

if we are not! He is not trapped in your church building. He accompanies you home and is with you whatever you get up to! Then there is what we do when we are inside 'church'. How do many of us get our instructions in Christian life and theology? It is via the 'sermon', of course! Yet the sermon did not really catch on until the 4th Century AD, around the same time that Greek ideas were beginning to take grip on the church. This is no co-incidence. The origins are with the *Sophists*, itinerant speakers who, dressed in their finery, gave impressive monologues, either in the public squares or at exclusive dinner parties.

This tradition was still alive at the time when the Christian church was flourishing under the official patronage of the Christianised Roman empire. Many accomplished orators became Christians, and some became paid preachers in the church circuits of the day. This caught on, as these orators were skilled and polished in their art, masters of Greek rhetoric. Soon only these trained individuals were allowed to preach to the masses. The mass impartation of Christian knowledge became a one-way street, delivered only by those with training in Greek rhetoric and oratory. The sermons were known as *homilies*, a word that still survives in the church. Now we are not suggesting that there is no place in Christian life for the sermon. Far from it! Jesus himself preached, *the sermon on the mount* being a good example. And so did Peter and Paul, as recorded in Acts. Noah himself was called a 'preacher of righteousness' in 2 Peter 2:5, heading a whole line of biblical preachers who proclaimed God's word to the people. But there are sermons and there are 'sermons'. Done correctly, it has been God's favoured way of preaching the Word. But what about our *itching ears*?

Sermons or homilies are not always preached in accordance with the clear teaching of Scripture. There are plenty of 'preachers' who have more in common with the Greek Sophists than those biblical teachers who bring the word alive for the sustenance of needy and hungry sheep. (Remember Jesus' insistent call to the apostle Peter – "Feed my sheep"). The modern-day Sophists command many pulpits, and we think particularly of some of the televangelists! Showmanship and cleverness may become the priorities, rather than a humble and powerful exposition of God's word. As Christians we must learn discernment, at the very least. So how do we do this? When the preacher lifts his hands to God, we should look to see how many fingers are pointing back to him, figuratively speaking of course! This is not an attack on any particular church or minister. It is just a warning about what has gone wrong in some parts of the church. There are plenty of *Sophists* out there and, as we conclude this chapter, we will outline how they get away with it!

Remember *Plato's big idea*, that the soul and the 'spiritual' are good and the body and the 'physical' is bad. We have seen how this gave us celibate priests, afraid of interactions with the 'dirty' physical world. It gave us the *clergy* and the *laity*, a separation between 'spiritual' people and 'physical' people. It also gave us professional 'preachers' copying the Greek model of the Sophists. Today we live in a church made up of 38,000 denominations. This has mostly happened because different Christians, at different times, and in different places, adopted their own way of deciding what the Bible says. We have heard those TV preachers: *The Bible says*! *Thus says the Lord*! *The Lord is doing a new thing*! *Here's what you must do to get blessed*!

Yet in reality hasn't God it so easy for us? He put the whole thing in one book. There it all is, everything you need to find salvation and meaning and live your lives in a godly way, available in just a single book, small enough to fit in your pocket. The Bible has a single author – God. We know Him, we can trust Him – if we cannot trust Him then the issue is with us, not with God! So why are there so many ways of reading it? It's back to the Greeks, I'm afraid – back to Plato. His ideas affected how people read the Bible. Some of those Church Fathers looked at the Bible and decided that they were going to interpret it using techniques from Greek philosophy, married with insights from early Christian tradition and other writings. As we discovered in Chapter 3, people all too easily select a personalised and comfortable hermeneutic, often choosing *eisegesis* (reading into texts to 'discover' meanings) rather than the safer *exegesis* (reading out of Scripture what the writer and the context clearly demand).

The principle that the Sophists followed was that the Bible contained *three levels of meaning*, corresponding to the body, soul and spirit. We can see the influence of Plato here, and the beginning of eisegesis. The early church leaders in the post apostolic period considered that the 'body' level of interpretation, *the plain literal meaning of the text*, was for the simple minded, whereas the 'soul' and more particularly the 'spirit' levels of meaning were for *more enlightened* readers. So, apparently, only the special 'spiritual' ones could read the 'spiritual' messages hidden within the Holy Scripture! The technique used most of all was the same one already used in the study of Greek texts, such as those of Homer. This tool was known as *allegory* and the damage it did to understanding of the biblical text was extreme. Allegory – a key concept, so it is worth labouring the point in order to fully understand it in every way. It is defined as a way of representing a situation, giving it a meaning that is not a literal meaning. We can cite a well known example as a great way to get a grip on this idea: George Orwell's *Animal Farm* was an allegory of the Soviet era of Stalin in the pre-war years. Whereas readers may have a hate figure in Napoleon the pig, there is a greater hate figure implied, being Josef Stalin himself. So, if we take the story *literally*, it is just a story about talking animals on a farm, but *allegorically* it is a political satire.

One big question we need to ask is whether the author intended to create an allegory and, if so, what point was he making? In George Orwell's case, the allegory was clear and unambiguous. So what about the Bible? Well, we know Who the author is – God Himself. So when the Church Fathers went through the text of the Bible, they had to be sure that, if they saw allegory, then *the author Himself would need to be in agreement*. And, if He wasn't, then they were treading on very dangerous ground indeed! The scene was now set. Because of the demands of the Platonic worldview in preferring the spiritual over the physical, *spiritual meanings were sought*, even in Bible passages that were obviously meant to be taken literally. A free-for-all was now created, allowing Christian teachers, right up to the current day, to be able to bend and coax God's word to say whatever they wanted it to say! That is the legacy of the infiltration of Greek philosophy into Christian theology.

The ideas of Plato were mixed in with what has been presented by way of a significant amount of church teaching down the centuries, thanks to those Church Fathers, from Clement and Origen, through to Augustine and Thomas Aquinas. The church is far more 'Greek' in its outlook than people have imagined. And this is not a side issue, but very much a key battleground for the truth, even today. Indeed it is not so much a battle, but a full-on war for the Christian heart and mind, although most Christians are blissfully unaware of the conflict.

So where does that leave us – is there any good news?
There is indeed good news! It is the *gospel*, literally the 'good news'. And where is this good news to be found? In the Bible. Christians really do need to get back to basics, back to their Bibles. We need to be like the Bereans and examine and test everything: **Now the Bereans were of more noble character than the Thessalonians, for they received the message with great eagerness and examined the Scriptures every day to see if what Paul said was true** (Acts 17:11). So please don't take my word for it. Examine

the Scriptures, not the traditions of men. And God will surely bless you as you do so.

"Happy are those who have been invited to the wedding feast of the Lamb"

Chapter Six

OF ROOTS AND BRANCHES

A Church without God

I am prepared to be proved wrong on this! Just before this book was begun, in 2013, there were media reports on a new movement emerging in the English speaking world. This was the atheist 'Sunday Assembly', something that had been dubbed *the new face of atheism*. The premise was simple: atheists, especially those with any sort of church background, miss some elements of the certainties and joys that church life brings, including the social interaction with local communities, and could hardly ignore the pesky reality that church adherence does seem to bring a range of social benefits, including health benefits, to adherents. So, the question became how to mimic the benefits without making way for any idea of God? The answer: *the godless church*, or the 'Sunday Assembly'. Billed on its UK website as 'part-foot stomping show, part-atheist church', it was proving sufficiently popular in 2013 that arriving at the Assembly early on a Sunday morning was advised, so as to be sure of getting a seat!

It is easy to see how those who don't believe in God might find such a group appealing. Going to a meeting led by two comics, where people sing along to Cyndi Lauper and Fleetwood Mac, listen to homilies on themes such as 'wonder' and 'play' and chat over a cup of tea afterwards, would inevitably be popular. It was direct and unabashed mimicry of the typical modern church. Brainchild of UK comedians Sanderson Jones and Pippa Evans, the gathering was not, it was claimed, about being *anti-religion*, but rather to encourage the non-religious to live a good life. 'Our mission is to help everyone find and fulfil their potential,' said Sanderson Jones.[1] The motto of The Sunday Assembly was 'Live better, help often, wonder more'.

Following its inaugural London meeting in January 2013, the growth of the movement was notable – within a few months there were two 'services' a month and ambitious plans to expand and extend. From London the Assembly reached out to Exeter, Brighton, Bristol and Southend. Interest was not confined to the UK. By April 2013, Pippa Evans had visited Australia to oversee the launch of the Sunday Assembly Melbourne. A sense of community and social action were to be hallmarks of this new movement. So, in what way am I prepared to be proved wrong? Only in this: I suspect that the movement will not become a replacement or serious 'rival' to Christianity, and that the early excitement will wane. I would be surprised if it maintains itself for more than a few years. Furthermore, in mimicking churches, these Assemblies are certain to encounter a sad reality of church life. That is, sooner or later, there will emerge dissension, argument and controversy! The Sunday Assembly phenomenon was, however, interesting and noteworthy at the time of writing. Whereas parts of the church in the early 21st Century seemed to believe that the church was (or should be) an extension of the welfare state, there was a clear movement from the other direction; atheists mimicking church and also wanting to be involved in 'good works'. How soon would it be before the two became indistinguishable? In the light of everything we have explored so far in this book, the answer was, surely, not very long, as some church-attending Christians also showed interest in the early success and philosophy of the Sunday Assembly.

---

[1] Report on Premier Radio website, June 2013.

A sub-theme of this book is: to what extent is a completely godless church in the offing? In 2 Timothy 3:1–5, as the apostle Paul speaks of the godless church in the last days, he tells Timothy that he needs to do two things: (1) understand that in the last days troublesome times will come; and (2) keep his distance from false religion. The warning applies as much to us today. Let us look at this key verse 5 in three translations.

...they will hold to the outward form of our religion, but reject its real power. Keep away from such people. (GNB)

...having a form of godliness but denying its power. Have nothing to do with them. (NIV)

...Having a form of godliness, but denying the power thereof: from such turn away (AV)

On this occasion the GNB seems to have the edge! However I will also draw readers' attention to the *One New Man Bible*, a fresh 2011 translation by William J Morford. In this regard and with due focus on the original texts, Morford renders v. 5 as:

...having an appearance of reverence, but denying the power of it: so you must continually turn away from these things.

Morford's translation seems to hit the proverbial nail on the head as regards the rebel church. For a time this church appears to be reverent towards God, but in so many ways, in its actions and in its teaching, it denies the power of the gospel message, by eisegesis of the gospel to encompass ideas not plainly taught in Scripture. For fifty or more years there have been stories circulating about priests and vicars who do not actually believe in God, although we may speculate that this phenomenon dates back, perhaps, to the earliest of times. Some of these clerics duly resign their job whilst others soldier on, going through the motions, in the expectation of drawing some sort of pension. But Paul tells Timothy, as he tells us, that we must **continually turn away from these things**. This is not a one-time adjustment for believing Christians. It is a challenge that will emerge again and again, like a dormant virus, to wreak havoc when it arises. Or, like Japanese knotweed in a garden, something that is virtually impossible to remove unless the most radical surgery is undertaken.

The Choice is God's

Allowing, as we explored in chapter 5, that the church has definitely trodden a path that was not in accordance with God's original intention, sometimes by adopting Greek philosophical ideas that have coloured its thinking ever since, just what is it that the church has lost, and can it regain it? Should it even try to regain it?

For the past forty years there have been periodic calls amongst different churches to return to a New Testament type of church, to recover a purity and simplicity that self-evidently has been lost. There seems perhaps to be one great flaw in this otherwise laudable desire: it ignores the fact that the apostolic church was far from perfect. A large proportion of the text of Acts and the epistles concern controversies and heresies – and the need to combat the latter. We can learn all we need to know about the sort of church we should be by reading the Scriptures – especially the New Testament – but to 'return' *back to the future*, as it were, may be just too simplistic an answer. Besides, the Bible in its prophecy is adamant that the church will not be ready for the return of the Lord – and to that extent (only) we might declare that the church cannot be 'fixed'. But the good news is that there is a pattern set out in the New Testament and that we can know the **mind of Christ** – both to honour Him because we love Him, and to 'see things' more consciously in the way that Jesus sees things.

The other part of the good news is that God has always said He will preserve for Himself a remnant – a sub-set of people who will remain steadfast and loyal to the very end. Who are these people, the remnant? It would be all too tempting and all too comforting to say: "Well, it's *my* denomination, of course!" Few of us as denominational Christians would be likely to remain for long in our church if we truly believed it to be thoroughly bad, characterised by false teaching or ungodly practices. So we typically will think that it is the *other* denominations that need to change, to become more like my denomination, with which I am, generally speaking, comfortable. But we must each one of us challenge ourselves: is our denomination a good benchmark of what the Lord wanted and intended? If the previous five chapters have any resonance with readers, then the answer could well be no! Whilst it is logically true that some denominations are measurably better than others, in the sense of being more faithful to the teachings of Jesus, is this all there is to it? What was it, precisely, that the very earliest Christians had, that gave them a spiritual vitality and an assurance, and indeed a holiness that was remarkable, and that we no longer have? And is that missing ingredient recoverable?

Astute Christian readers will have a sense of where this question might be heading. For the past fifty or sixty years the church has continually worried about its apparent unstoppable decline, and wondered why an all-powerful God would seemingly ignore His saints' heartfelt prayers for revival. Is Peter Sammons about to unveil his *big idea* as to what that elusive missing ingredient is, and, as have so many commentators before, pronounce *the* way to mend the fortunes of the church, if only everyone else would adopt his idea? I can perhaps assuage your concern on this score!

The purpose of this book is not to promote a sure-fire way of saving the church. And we will not engage in such promotion for two very good reasons:

1. The Lord was crystal clear that not all of the church would be ready for Him when He returns in glory. So anything I say would inevitably fall on largely stony ground – the church *will* rebel – for **a time is coming**... as we saw in chapter 5.

2. It is to *individual believers* that any message must primarily be directed, rather than to institutions with their vested interests and their innate conservatism (*we* have it right so why should *we* change?)

Before I answer my own question (*is that missing ingredient recoverable*?) I would first observe that for following Jesus, quite simply, the prerequisite is to: "**Repent, for the Kingdom of heaven is near**" (Matthew 4:17; Mark 1:15). *Repentance toward God*, and *believing and trusting in Jesus* as the Son of God, and the associated *new birth* are necessary in order to see the kingdom (see John chapter 3). Without these crucial things, everything else we might say is entirely wasted. *Repentance* means a change of mind and direction, a turning away from sin, and also ceasing from depending on our own 'good works'. It also calls for true contrition. Thus repentance is *essential*. We can be delighted as we assert, with total assurance, that the Holy Spirit breaks through and breaks down any hindering barriers of ignorance, prejudice and resistance, so repentance is entirely possible for anyone.

What we are about to explore together is not the only answer, but I would go so far as to say that *it is an essential sub-element in health and vitality for the individual believer*, and by extension, for the wider church. What we are about to explore is *not* something that, taken in isolation, guarantees that all will be sweetness and light, closeness and security for the church, guaranteeing that the Bride will be ready and waiting, properly attired, awaiting her Groom to take her to Himself. *But what we are about to explore is a badly needed corrective that will help us to detoxify from the damaging excesses of Greek thinking – that Greek mindset – that have afflicted the church from its earliest days*, and should enable the individual Christian, if not the wider church, to think aright about the many issues that confront the church in these latter days, and in this decidedly post-Christian culture. Thinking aright actually means *thinking biblically*.

Is it an accident that Jesus was a Jew? Would it have been quite the same if Jesus had been a New Zealander, or a Chinaman, an Indian, a Zimbabwean or a Brazilian? Of course it was no accident. We have to do away with such pointless human speculation! The fact is that *God Himself* chose the Jews and it is not for us to argue with what he sovereignly does. In the next few paragraphs, we will review some of the key texts that shed light on this matter. The numbers in parentheses refer to specific texts which are included for ease of reference in Appendices 4 and 5:

The first book of the Bible, Genesis, reveals that God chose to make Abraham into a great nation (1). The descendants of Abraham, the Hebrews (Jews), would establish the nation of Israel to become a people of God's own possession (2).

The Bible says that the Jews were chosen to be a blessing to all the nations of the world (1). God's love was settled on His *Chosen People*, for His own possession, and never to be irredeemably rejected (3). The same passages that tell us that God chose the Hebrews also assert that God does not show partiality and commands the Jews to love other peoples (4). The Old Testament indicates that the Jews were not chosen because of their righteousness, since they were 'a stubborn people'. (5) The main way that the Jews would be a blessing to all peoples of the world was that the Messiah would be born through the line of King David. Beginning with the third chapter of Genesis, the Old Testament reveals progressively that the Messiah would be the Saviour of the world [*see Appendix 4 for a key selection*]. These prophecies specifically state that the Messiah would be God in human flesh, (6) who would also be the Son of God (7). The Messiah would establish the new covenant (8) and would die as the ultimate sacrifice for the sins of all people (9).

The above is offered as a brief biblical introduction to two ideas that are controversial: first, that God's choice of Israel is for all time; and, second, that His choice has implications for the church today. On the basis that tens of millions of words have been expended examining this subject in the past fifty or more years, I am not going to try to 'defend' the foregoing except to rebut one common and increasingly popular argument: this is the belief that we are to *read into* these biblical passages the idea that the church has become the new Israel, so the biblical passages are all allegory about the future church. The hermeneutic underlying that view would require that we do not read these texts in their plainest possible reading but that we eisegete the idea that 'Israel' means 'church' which would mean that the church has inherited all the blessings associated with Israel. And this includes, should there be any specific geographic claim relating to the land of Israel, that the church has inherited (if anyone has inherited) the 'title deeds' to the Land, thus excluding the Jewish people for all time. Such ideas rejoice in the title of 'Replacement Theology', suggesting that the church has replaced Israel in God's affections.

My rebuttal is two-fold: firstly, if this is really true, do we not think there would be just one text in the whole Bible that expressed this idea *plainly*, since the idea is clearly intended to abrogate all the texts set out at length in Appendices 4 and 5? And, secondly, the people who make this claim seem to be unaware that whenever God provided a prophetic blessing to Israel in the Old Testament, He almost always brackets it with an associated curse linked to disobedience.

If the church has inherited all the blessings of Israel, has it not also inherited the associated curses? Whilst most *replacement theologians* seem reluctant to acknowledge the term 'replacement theology', it certainly describes succinctly their beliefs.

This book is not the place to attempt to fully resolve these questions, which have been more ably dealt with by other Christian writers in a biblically faithful and astute way. I will mention just three recent books that deal with this whole area.[2] Alex Jacobs' introductory text *Receive the Truth* poses 20 FAQs in this area and then provides a simple, straightforward biblical evaluation of each. *The Case For Enlargement Theology*, by the same author, is probably the leading text in this area. This is a detailed theological treatise and presupposes its readers will have some serious reverence for the Word, and some prior theological understanding. In other words it is probably not a text for absolute beginners. 'Enlargement Theology' is proffered by Alex Jacob as a term to describe the enlargement of some aspects of God's ancient covenantal relationship with His chosen people, the Hebrews, to encompass all believers in Jesus, *Yeshua*. The third book is *Israel in the New Testament* by David Pawson, which traces the key distinctions between Israel and the church, in the course of Bible Studies on a number of relevant books of the New Testament. Each of these books will help to set the scene on a very important debate.

As God alone is sovereign, we need to accept that the choice is His, and His alone. God has done something special as regards the Hebrew people and this has continuing implications for the church today. Jesus was a Jew. He lived and taught as a Jew. Certainly 64 of the 66 books of the Bible were written by Jews. But the church has de-Judaized down through history as a conscious policy, continually denying its Hebraic root (Romans 12:18) and the implications that flow

---

[2] See full details in the Further Reading section.

from it. The result is replacement theology and the church's frequent bouts of persecution against Jewish communities. I will not attempt to defend these controversial and very over-simplified propositions, as so many writers have spilled ink on this battleground in the past hundred years. There is plenty of material out there for the interested reader.

Make your mind up

The question of precisely which of God's covenants are still in place and which have been 'replaced' is still keenly debated. In Appendix 3 (*A Covenant God*) readers will find a simple framework within which to consider these matters and pursue their own Bible study if they have questions and issues around this specific matter of the church and Israel. Plenty of 'theologians' will offer alternative views – and opposing views – so if readers doubt this author then they can find many other guides in this area! I would suggest, however, that not having a considered opinion on this vital subject is no longer a tenable position for the serious Christian, especially when set against the backdrop of a rebellious church. In Appendix 3, readers will find a Table which suggests that Covenants numbered 1, 2, 4 and 5 are still 'in force' and, although it is not a covenant in the same vein, what I have called Covenant 0 (God's promise made to mankind through Adam) similarly remains 'in force' in perpetuity. It is the covenant made with Moses that the writer to the Hebrews regarded as the 'old covenant' that has been changed. In the Epistle to the Hebrews (at 8:6) we learn that the covenant of Jesus – the 'new covenant' is superior to the old (Mosaic) covenant (8:13). Why is all this important? Because it suggests to us, then, that God's ongoing purposes for Israel remain, as the other covenants continue to inform us.

So, what does this critical and emotive debate have to do with the rebel church? Is this not an entirely different – and stand-alone – subject? A careful study of the passages of Scripture relating to the return of Jesus and the end-time events prophesied, not least in the Book of Revelation, will discover that the place of Israel in God's plan is extremely significant. That is at least one reason to declare that this is a highly relevant field of Scripture study. Furthermore, events in our times, including the recent history of the rebel church and the growth of persecution of Christians, fit the whole thrust of the prophetic warnings about events that we are seeing unfold in the world. It all fits together. So we do have to make up our minds on this emotive subject.

It is this writer's contention that as the established churches fall into what might have to be called final apostasy and identify *totally* with this world and with its agenda (even if it strenuously denies this!) then those who are true to Jesus – those who know the voice of the Good Shepherd – will joyfully continue in their love for the Lord, and indeed will experience that *phileo* love in ways that will be deeper and more satisfying than anything experienced by His church since the earliest days of the apostolic church. What a wonderful prospect that is!

In addition, a refreshed relationship of individual believer to the Lord can usher in the wonderful prospect of reaching out to unbelievers in ways reminiscent of those triumphs of the early church, when people were eager to hear the good news of Jesus, and were willing to follow Him as disciples whatever the cost. (And we remember that the cost of discipleship to believers then, as it remains today in many parts of the world, was enormously high. A cost that could entail loss of family, home, friendships, citizenship and even of life itself. And yet they joyfully responded to His gentle call: *Come and follow me*).

There is also another area in which it is important that we should turn our minds to Scriptural truths which may often have been ignored. We saw in chapter 5 that the thinking of the church has too often been influenced by aspects of

'Greek' philosophy which can sometimes tend to obscure the things of God.

It is helpful to approach Scripture with some understanding of the Hebraic ways of thinking into which Jesus ministered. Let us be very clear first of all about this: *Every word that Jesus Himself uttered was the very word of God. Jesus heard perfectly what the Father said, and moved and spoke with perfect inspiration of the Holy Spirit.* So we must be extremely wary of trying to characterise or categorise him and his words as though they were culturally determined. We are not, as it were, to try to analyse the 'psychology' of Jesus and say that it was either 'Hebraic' or 'Greek'. To do so would make no sense at all, and would fall into the same trap as the liberal critics who take huge liberties in analysing and deconstructing what they read in the Bible. Jesus did speak to some Gentiles and His words to them were invariably just as perfectly inspired and full of wisdom and divine insight as when He was speaking to His fellow-Jews. God Himself was incarnate as a Jewish man, but was not bound or restricted in His words by that identity. As we have noted, the words of the Son perfectly reveal the Father's will, and they apply universally and are relevant to people of all races on earth. They speak to everyone exactly as they stand.

It is also interesting to note that the Greek/Hebraic distinction which no doubt has some validity, is not the last word on the subject. There is more to be said. In the New Testament itself, some Greek concepts are used. We could start by thinking of the *logos* concept in the Gospel of John chapter 1. We could continue with the mind/body distinction deployed by Paul – and so on.

With those caveats, it is certainly the case that we can usefully learn a great deal more than Christians usually know today about first century Jewish thought and culture, simply because that helps us to understand some of the concepts used in the New Testament, and to see more clearly the perfect way in which Jesus fulfilled the Torah. That is important to us who now live 'in Him' because he has met all the requirements of the Law for *us* as much as for Jewish believers. Every Gentile believer has reason to be thankful that the Saviour in whom we now live and move kept the Ten Commandments for us. It is because He was perfectly righteous that those he has justified are treated as though we were. Unless we know that, as Paul explained it in Romans, we will not see the wonderful truth that both Jewish believer and Gentile believer alike are justified on the same basis as Abraham was – by grace through faith. It is good that we should understand how Jesus made that possible for all.

We live in a "pick 'n' mix" culture nowadays. This culture is marked by what many call *postmodernism*, a rejection of certainties and absolute truth and thus a sworn enemy of biblical Christianity. Postmodernism allows us to decide what *seems right for us* and leaves us to create a comfortable framework around which to construct our life's journey. It is relativist and humanistic, and cannot accommodate the notion of revealed truth – the Creator God intervening in the world He has made. It is the latest expression of a process that started late in the 1st Century AD, when the Jewish disciples of Jesus had died off and the reins of Christianity were taken up by Gentile adherents of the Greek philosophers, mainly Plato and Aristotle. Their legacy is a 'mainstream' Christianity riddled with a pagan Greek mindset that still influences us even today, although most of us cannot easily identify it. The *dualism* of Plato and the *rationalism* of Aristotle have worked together to colour many presuppositions we bring to the faith. One aspect is the way we tend to put *self* at the centre, rather than God. Yet our thinking and living should be centred on the Lord Jesus: **Then Jesus said to his disciples, "If anyone would come after me, he must deny himself and take up his cross and follow me. For whoever wants to save his life will lose it, but whoever loses his life for me will find it** (Matthew 16:24–25).

Is the so-called 'Greek mindset' one of the driving forces behind *humanism* and *individualism*, putting man at the centre, usurping God's rightful place? Does it elevate our rational mind, processing the world through its 'filtering system' and rejecting anything that cannot be figured out or discerned through the five senses of sight, hearing, touch, smell and taste? These are proper questions to ask.

The gospel speaks to any and every culture and ethnic group, overcoming all barriers, as indeed it did in the early church. It certainly helps to know what some of those barriers are, and the contribution of those theologians who encourage us to explore our Hebraic root has been to help us to see what we are missing if we confine our ways of thinking to the rationalistic approaches which have marked so much Western thought and culture.

Having affirmed that, in truth it is not so much the world and its mix of cultures and philosophies that is the problem for the preaching of the gospel in this day and age. It is the *rebellious church* that must concern us, and the extent to which it has interacted with and adopted the culture that surrounds it. It has been rightly said that the early church got into the world, but later the world got into the church. God knows everything and it should occasion no surprise when we see that much of the New Testament – a great part of the Epistles in particular – addresses precisely this point. Worldly ways and standards got in and had to be brought under the discipline (discipleship) that should be a normative aspect of the life of a fellowship. Read Jude, for example. At once we see what was already happening, and sound ways of handling the problem were established. James gives us the principle:

You adulterous people, don't you know that friendship with the world is hatred toward God? Anyone who chooses to be a friend of the world becomes an enemy of God (James 4:4).

The whole thesis of this book is that the church itself is in increasing rebellion (against the rule of God), and as in any situation of rebellion, we have to decide which side we are on!

Author Steve Maltz poses a number of questions and invites us to do the same. The important questions that impact all of us who consider ourselves to be Christians are these:

- Surely there is more to my Christian walk than what I see around me in the church today?
- Why isn't there certainty in the church any more?
- Are we really experiencing what God had planned for us?

Maltz is one of a number of modern commentators who suggest that a *Hebraic* mindset may help us to answer these questions. These modern writers suggest it is time that we dig a little deeper, as did those Pharisees who confronted Jesus: **One of them, an expert in the law, tested him with this question: "Teacher, which is the greatest commandment in the Law?" Jesus replied: "'Love the Lord your God with all your heart and with all your soul and with all your mind.' This is the first and greatest commandment. And the second is like it: 'Love your neighbour as yourself.' All the Law and the Prophets hang on these two commandments"** (Matthew 22:35–40).

In this statement Jesus summarised the Ten Commandments, reducing them to their bare bones and declaring that they are first and foremost about love for God and also for our fellow man. This is not some wishy-washy dewy-eyed sentimentality. This is real, practical, get-your-hands-dirty love, expressed as devotion to God and reflected in our obedience to Jesus, and in the way we conduct ourselves with our fellow men. Love for God is expressed in our worship of Him alone, and in our respect for His name, by not swearing or blaspheming with it. Love for our fellow men, our 'neighbour', is expressed in honouring our parents, not engaging in murder, or sleeping around, or stealing, lying or being covetous.

This is familiar stuff. We know we should love God, putting Him centre of everything we do. Yet the *dualism* that has infiltrated the church from 'Greek' thinking has persuaded us to think that we can divide our lives into *the spiritual* and *the secular*, and that God is somehow only involved in our 'spiritual' moments, in church on a Sunday or during prayer meetings or Bible study. So much of our 'Christianity' is about *separation*, whether in our practices, lifestyles, doctrines, or even in the way we read the Bible. We should love our neighbour by acting in such a way that others will see Jesus reflected in our lives, but sadly we don't always do that. Our words and actions don't always match up. The thread of *rationalism* in the church has given rise to our endless quarrelling over secondary issues which have often resulted in schisms, loss of fellowship and frequent church splits. The *daddy* of church splits was, of course, that original schism between the Western and Eastern churches. The world generally sees Christians as a divided, quarrelsome people, rather than the redeemed representatives of God on earth. Knowing that parts of the institutional church are today in increasing rebellion against the Spirit – the whole thesis of this book – then surely it is time to change?

So what is Hebraic thinking? It can be contrasted with Greek thinking in the following statements:
The 'Greek' mind says that man is at the centre of life; the 'Hebraic' mind says that God is at the centre of life. The 'Greek' mind says that the things of God must be deduced from our logical minds; the 'Hebraic' mind says that the things of God can only be understood by faith and revelation. The 'Greek' mind says that we should strive for knowledge about God; the 'Hebraic' mind says that we should know God.

Readers should take time to ponder the above. Steve Maltz explores these ideas exhaustively in his book "*How the Church Lost the Truth*" (see the Further Reading section at the end of this book). But for those of us who are concerned about the rebellious church, in these ideas we begin to see the possibility for worthwhile change. Let us reflect for a moment on that last one again: *The Greek mind says that we should strive for knowledge **about** God; the Hebraic mind says that we should **know** God.*

Think about it. The suggestion being made by some writers is that the 'Greek' part of us inclines us towards building ourselves a whole library of books, podcasts and sermons that help to develop a 'systematic theology' about God. Now that's not necessarily bad! There is good kind of systematic biblical theology, which simply sets out clearly what the Bible teaches, arranged by topics (as Wayne Grudem does so well, for example), showing the reader what God has revealed in His written Word and drawing together related themes to help us in our study. The objection being made is to the more *speculative* kind of systematics. The writers who are encouraging us to make this Greek/Hebraic distinction would say that the 'Hebraic' part of us inclines us to drop to our knees and ask Him to teach us His ways. The 'Hebraic' mind can be expressed in these verses in James:

What good is it, my brothers, if a man claims to have faith but has no deeds? Can such faith save him? (James 2:14).

Who is wise and understanding among you? Let him show it by his good life, by deeds done in the humility that comes from wisdom (James 3:13).

Whilst Christians rightly assert that salvation is by grace through faith, a faith that does not lead on to good works is ultimately dead. As the Lord Jesus Himself said, in two different contexts, it is those who *do the will of His Father* who will be counted as His brothers and sisters (Matthew 7:21 and 12:50). The will of the Father is that we love our neighbour as ourselves. But, before any 'liberal' theologian (and we are forced to adopt that term as an unfortunate catch-all for the rebellious mindset now so prevalent in today's church) says "I do lots of good works – I help poor people" and believe that they are therefore "safe" on this basis, we must look at the other side of the coin from Jesus: John 14:15; 14:21 and 14:23 all make it crystal clear that *obedience* is paramount. It is in this area of obedience that the modern church, in its actions and in its teachings, is now in outright rebellion. The day I wrote this paragraph, I heard on the radio the following from a well-known, and mainstream, Catholic theologian: "sin means social inequality". It is well known that many Catholics are involved in so-called liberation theology, but his comment is surely representative of 'liberal' thought across the church spectrum. It is thought by many that the moral law is out of date, and that we are free to live our lives in defiance of God's commandments providing we are doing socially useful things. I think we can safely say, no matter how earnestly this belief may be held by some 'church people', that God does not agree.

Of roots and branches (1)
This has been a gentle and deliberative introduction to the idea that those who will remain faithful to Jesus are inevitably going to have to divorce themselves from the mindset of the world. This has always been true and has been widely recognised. But Christians still have no real key to unlock *what this means in practice*. Getting back to the Bible has always been a part of it, but have there not been 'revivals' and 'outpourings' in the past? Yet today we have a church that glories in its rebellions. *Surely things today are materially different than at any time in the history of the church*. And as we learned in 2 Timothy 4:3 **a time is coming**....

There seem to be two elements to this idea of acquiring a 'Hebraic' outlook. The first is that it understands and acknowledges that the Christian church consists of, in the apostle Paul's words, wild olive branches that are in-grafted into the Hebrew root (Romans 11:17–18). This is something of which we are to take note and in which we are to delight. How could we do otherwise? Paul has pointed this out for a very good reason, so it would be foolish to ignore something that is clearly rather important! The second is simply that our understanding of the interconnectedness of the Old and New Testaments will be enhanced and blessed by God. This in turn will give us greater assurance in His Word, and in turn, in His promises. And that, in turn, will sustain us through the harsh times that lie ahead. I would venture to suggest, as well, that it would tend to make us identify more as citizens of the kingdom of God rather than as denominational adherents. We have seen that the real church is the fellowship of believers, and we should not stop meeting with other believers, but there is much in the often bureaucratic, administrative structures that we can sit rather lightly to!

A right relationship to our root is a healthy thing. But like all good and healthy things in the Bible, the devil is out there to frustrate, obfuscate and deceive. Accordingly there is some frankly foolish and divisive teaching around what has been called the 'Hebraic Roots Movement'. Somehow we need to connect with the good, and resist the bad in this whole area, and it is to this that we turn our attention in the next two chapters.

"Happy are those who have been invited to the wedding feast of the Lamb"

Chapter Seven

20–20 VISION

Phileo Yeshua – I love Jesus

The heading of this section *Phileo Yeshua* is simply a linkage of the classical Greek word *phileo* – the word for that strong love which involves warmth and affection toward another person – with the Hebrew name *Yeshua*, which we render as 'Jesus' in the English language. We should have *phileo* love towards Jesus. (Though of course we remember that we are also to 'agape' Jesus, as Jesus memorably invited Peter to articulate. Helpfully, what *our agape love toward Jesus* should lead to has been defined for us in John's Gospel [14:15 and 14:23]. Quite simply: for us to express *agape* [love] to Jesus involves obeying Him – doing what He tells us; keeping His words. That could scarcely be simpler.)

Phileo Yeshua may be a helpful term, enabling us to articulate one of the kinds of love that we have for our Jewish Saviour. In the previous chapter we were challenged to consider whether as individual Christians we need to 'detox' as it were from aspects of the 'Greek' mindset which is the cultural heritage that has been predominant in Europe, and attempt to acquire a more 'Hebraic' way of seeing things. In this chapter we explore what this might mean in practice. One generalisation is necessary, and once again I apologise in advance for I know it will upset at least some: the church, generally speaking, does not like the Jews. In fact, generally speaking, it *dislikes* the Jews and in our day the various 'mainstream' churches are aligning ever more decidedly against the modern State of Israel with the – perhaps convenient – excuse that it is supporting the Palestinians. Could it be that the mainstream church has found a fresh *cause celebre* or even a *casus belli* to act as a fig-leaf for its age-old dislike of the Jews and Judaism? Some might think this an unduly harsh question. If so, I invite those readers to reflect on this in their own minds but, allowing that a time will come when large numbers of Jewish people will put their trust in Yeshua,[1] the precise relationship between believing Jew and believing Gentile will become an increasingly pressing issue in the future. If God has a purpose in Israel and a purpose for the Jewish people, will a rebel church align with God, or with the world? That is perhaps a rhetorical question!

So what do we mean by Hebraic thought? We can explore what Hebraic thought is, by stating what it is not! It is not a church or even a para church. It is not the last word in understanding Hebraic things. It is not a new religion and it is not a call to become Jewish! With the church ever bolder in its rebellion, individual believers have no option but to consider their allegiance: are they faithful to Jesus or to 'the [institutional] church'? Unfortunately the choice is becoming that stark. An increasing number of churches, especially some independent ones, are showing an interest in facing forwards and girding themselves for the battles ahead. Many of these recognise that detoxifying from Greek thinking is an essential prerequisite. If the adoption of a more Hebraic mindset has one outcome above all others, it should be to encourage each one of us to go back to our Bible!

The basic starting point in acquiring a more Hebraic outlook is simply to recognize that the church emerged from Judaism and that the *new covenant* is for Jew and Gentile alike. (See again Appendix 3 in this regard). The fact that Christianity emerged from Judaism is not a coincidence – it is part of God's overall plan for mankind. Generally,

---

[1] The Hebrew name for Jesus

Christians believe that the epoch of the new covenant began at the first coming of Yeshua (Jesus), who began His ministry with the words **"The time is fulfilled, and the kingdom of God is at hand; repent and believe in the gospel"** (Mark 1:15). Christians believe that Jesus is the mediator of the new covenant, and that His blood shed at the crucifixion is the required seal of that new covenant. As Yeshua said: **"this cup that is poured out for you is the new covenant in my blood"** (Luke 22:20). As discussed in the previous chapter, the new covenant does extinguish the old Mosaic covenant but leaves the other covenants in place (those with Noah, Abraham and David). The new covenant is seen to enlarge upon the older covenants, extending to new covenant believers blessings promised to the Hebrews. Of someone who seeks a more Hebraic understanding we can say these things:

- We rejoice in the in-grafting of the wild olive to the Hebrew root.
- We seek to learn from Hebrew thinking.
- We do not seek to 'Judaize' the church but we do seek the blessing associated with praying for the Hebrew people in all their travails and needs.

Those who seek to think more Hebraically recognise (and increasingly rejoice in seeing themselves as being part of) 'One New Man' – the redeemed humanity, Jew and Gentile alike, saved by Yeshua (Ephesians 2:15). The 2011 *One New Man* translation of the Bible uses Ephesians 2:15 as its inspiration and motif. In this book we seek to encourage all believers to see Yeshua Ha'Mashiach (Jesus the Messiah or Jesus the Christ) as a Jewish Man within His Hebraic hinterland, as well as the better known Saviour of all mankind. The essential biblical theology around salvation remains that salvation is a gift of God's grace through faith in the finished work of Yeshua Ha'Mashiach (Jesus Christ) on the cross (Ephesians 2:8–9). Messiah's (Christ's) death fully accomplished justification through faith and redemption from sin. Messiah (Christ) died in our place (Romans 5:8–9) and bore our sins in His own body (1 Peter 2:24).

Frequently Asked Questions about the Hebrew Root and its implications for Believers

* What is the Hebrew Root?

The Hebrew Root is simply a way of describing the idea that the church is in-grafted as wild branches into the "olive tree" of God's elect. The apostle Paul was crystal clear that this is the case. (Romans 11:17–21, in particular is the key text here although all of Romans chapters 9, 10 and 11 should be read to get a biblical understanding of this). The church is not an independent or free-wheeling 'religion' – it is 'rooted'. When the roots of a plant suffer then the whole plant suffers. If we have dry roots our 'Christianity' will also be dry. In the same way we need to absorb spiritual nutrients through the root. The plant is not the root, nor is the root the plant. The two are inseparable.

In this book we argue that the church has artificially separated root from plant (or root from in-grafted branches) and suffered accordingly. Whilst there are numerous reasons for the churches' patchy record on obedience, holiness and praxis down through history, we would argue that artificial separation of root from branch has made the established churches 'proud' and too willing to ignore the Jewishness of their Saviour. The Bible reminds us that pride comes before a fall (Proverbs 16:18).

* Why is the Hebrew Root important?

The Hebrew Root is the root in which God's church is to grow (Romans 11:18). By acknowledging the Hebrew Root we express joyfully and confidently the uniqueness of Jesus, our Lord, who was born a Jew and lived in Israel during the period of his earthly ministry. We love Him as Saviour, we love Him as Shepherd, and we want to hear His voice ever more clearly. Part of that is to understand Jesus the Jewish teacher; Jesus the Jewish observer of the Law; Jesus the fulfilment of prophecy; Jesus within His Jewish community and hinterland. We should not knowingly neglect any aspect of Jesus our Lord – and His Jewishness is surely an aspect for which we need to make room in our appreciation of His beauty and His holiness.

* Is this a 'front' for Christian Zionism? Is this 'political'?

No. There are a range of views about what is loosely called Zionism (and incidentally what sort of Zionism does this question address? Is it Jewish Zionism? Or Jewish anti-Zionism? Is it Christian Zionism or Christian anti-Zionism? Is it Covenantal Zionism or Classical Zionism?). If your author was to choose a 'label' for his understanding of biblically true Zionism it would be Classical Zionism as adopted by the likes of Charles and John Wesley, the Puritan John Owen, Charles Simeon of Cambridge, Bishop Ryle of Liverpool, the Baptist Charles Haddon Spurgeon, Scots Andrew Bonar and Murray McCheyne. And also William Wilberforce, Lord Shaftesbury, and some politicians such as David Lloyd George, Winston Churchill, and even Harold Wilson. These are just some notable UK people who have subscribed to what is now called a 'classical' understanding of God's ongoing purposes for Israel. David Pawson's *Defending Christian Zionism* is a helpful short book exploring Classical Zionism.[2]

*Is the Hebrew Root divisive?

No – the very opposite. It unites believing Jew to believing Gentile. In a church riven with theological and praxis differences, and an often thoroughly rebellious church, the

[2] See Further Reading section at the end of this book for details

Hebrew Root will become increasingly important in the 21st Century in enabling believing-Christians (and believing Jews) to see and to strengthen those things that unite them rather than those things that divide them.

Is the Hebrew Root secondary?

It is arguable that the church has misunderstood its root from the time that the church ceased to be predominantly Jewish – in other words from the Second Century onwards. Once the church in effect became 'nationalised' (this is a gross over-simplification, but people will have a sense of what this means!) by the Roman Emperor Constantine, the church began to identify ever more closely with the State and this has been an issue for the church ever since. As the church relies more upon the State, arguably it relies less upon the Lord! Again this must be an over-simplification, but the history of the church and its close dealings with the State – with temporal 'powers' – has led to many compromises. How can we forget that the present 'Church of England' was born out of a divorce controversy!

Few Christians would argue that the church is in a healthy state. The emptying pews in the older established churches suggest it is unhealthy – and possibly terminally unhealthy. (This is not true of the non-denominational/independent churches nor of the church in the developing world). As we have seen elsewhere in this book, the Bible suggests that the church will seriously rebel against the Holy Spirit towards the end times – and we have no real idea as to how close we may be to those end times. The major themes explored earlier in this book suggest that wholesale rebellion is not far off. Steve Maltz's popular book *The Bishop's New Clothes* hits the nail on the head in its sub-title 'Has the Church sold out to the World?'

Remedying the defects of the past and addressing the rebellious nature of today's established churches is becoming an urgent priority for the true believer. The Bride must make Herself ready for the Groom (Revelation 19:7–8). It is arguable that a rediscovery of the Hebrew Root will be an important part of the church's preparation for His return in glory. So no, rediscovering our Hebrew Root and exploring it as a wonderful fresh vista showing us God's utter faithfulness is surely not secondary – indeed the reverse must be true. Re-evaluating our Hebraic inheritance may be a real key to facing the undoubted challenges that lie ahead – not least of which will be heightened persecution.

How does the Hebrew Root help us to draw closer to Jesus?

Simply by better recognizing and understanding our Saviour – the Jewish man, the itinerant Jewish teacher (rabbi), the true Yeshua, the incarnate Son of God who lived in our world as the perfect man and as the second 'Adam'. As God decided to place Yeshua into a recognized and indeed 'chosen' people-group, within their 'promised land', it is surely less than honouring to God for us to ignore the context into which our Lord was placed. It is the expectation of most Christians that at His triumphal return He will return to Jerusalem – to the place from which He left His disciples (see Acts chapter 1, and especially verse 11). These things surely speak of the importance of the Hebraic connection?

Which is the best/most reliable translation of the Bible?

Some translations are paraphrases and others use a theo-logical translation technique called dynamic equivalence. Whilst not ruling out the usefulness or efficacy of many translations, your author prefers the use of the New King James Version (NKJV) in the English language. The New International Version (NIV) is adequate. The older Authorised Version (the King James Version) can be razor sharp in its translation but its seventeenth century idiom will be a stumbling block for many, not least those for whom English is a foreign language. The brand new *One New Man* Bible is looking good, but is a more scholarly translation and its layout is at best challenging! This is really a translation for the serious student who seeks a good comparison with the common/popular versions. Your author merely cautions readers that not all Bible translations are equally good, and some adopt a rather partisan approach. It is important, then, to select a good, trusted version – and preferably not a paraphrase, which can in practice be rather misleading.

Ten things we should understand about the Hebrew root as Christians

1. Yeshua (Jesus) lived, died and was raised again as a Torah-observant Jew.
2. The earliest believers in Yeshua were not called 'Christians', they were called 'the people of the Way'. Is there a case for making the mental adjustment to consider ourselves, also, the people of the Way? (Jesus described Himself as the Way, the Truth and the Life in John 14:6.)
3. Of the 66 books that make up the Bible, certainly 64 were written by Jewish men. Is this a mere coincidence? The two that may have been an exception are the Gospel of Luke and the Acts of the Apostles, also written by Luke.
4. The Old Testament and the New Testament are intimately linked. There are over 900 prophecies in the Old Testament that point towards Yeshua (Jesus). To help understand our Lord's teachings we do well to understand more of the culture in which He ministered.
5. The New Covenant grows out of the Old Covenant. It is difficult to argue (as some attempt to) that the Old Covenant is extinguished by the New.
6. When our Lord returns physically in glory to this world, it is clear that He will return to Jerusalem.

7. It is powerfully argued that God's purposes for the Hebrew people continue to this day and that in God's good time the majority of Jewish people will also joyfully recognize and receive Yeshua (Jesus) as their Saviour.

8. There are powerful allusions to Yeshua (Jesus) throughout the Old Testament. This is often called 'typology' of Christ – one powerful such 'type' is the sense in which the Tabernacle in its physical 'furnishings' speaks directly of the life and ministry of Yeshua (Jesus).

9. However uncomfortable or controversial it may be, there are many who understand the return of the Jewish people to the lands we now call Israel as being a fulfilment of prophecy both in the New Testament and the Old Testament. Is the church ready to welcome Jewish believers in Yeshua?

10. The debt owed by individual Christians as chosen people (Ephesians 1:4) to the Chosen People, the Hebrews, is enormous, as set out in Romans 11.

The thoughts above are aimed to help stir up an interest in your Hebrew root, if you are a Gentile Christian. We are 'wild olive branches' grafted into the Hebrew root stock (see Romans 11:17). This is a vital allusion made by the apostle Paul; we need to understand it and to live it. We do not do so by becoming Jews! Such an idea is absurd and already dismissed by Paul (see Galatians 5:1–15).

Ten ways in which our discipleship will be blessed as we acquire a more Hebraic understanding

1. We see the beauty of Yeshua (Jesus) magnified. He was a real man living in a real community, among God's chosen people.

2. Jesus the real Man becomes the Saviour we understand more closely. We grow to love Him more intimately and want to serve Him more truly.

3. Our understanding of Scripture is enhanced and our trust of the Word is increased. This has to be a good thing as the world becomes increasingly hostile to 'Christianity' and as persecution increases.

4. Our desire for the Holy Spirit will be increased and we will want to be more open to Him.

5. We acquire insights that help us to resolve decisively some of the protracted questions that have impacted the church down through history, such as free will versus election.

6. We are better able to deal with the recurrent heresies that emerge and then re-emerge like a virus down through church history.

7. We can find ourselves freed from denominational theologies that can be destructive and divisive. We begin to acquire the mind of Christ rather than the minds of 'theologians'.

8. Our love for our neighbour will become more reflective of our love for the Lord – the two loves will tend to work 'hand in glove'. We will grow to love our Lord more, so our love for our neighbour increases.

9. We begin to see our walk with the Lord as being not so much a lifestyle adopted, but a reality that we joyfully see affect every aspect of our lives – our discipleship is enhanced

10. Our gift of discernment will be strengthened.

There are no doubt other ways in which our discipleship will be blessed. But the above seem to be the most visible benefits of acknowledging and rejoicing in our Hebrew lineage.

Why is the Christian church too often such a poor witness to the Gospel?

There is an enemy out there (the Bible calls him the devil) who seeks to spoil and to destroy. He particularly likes to keep the church on its back-foot, focusing on side-issues rather than preaching the gospel of Yeshua (Jesus). One weapon in his arsenal is Greek philosophy. Greek philosophy is in sharp contrast to the certainties of Hebraic thought patterns. Hebraic thought patterns often allow us to see innumerable godly possibilities where Greek thought patterns restrict us only to 'logical' thought processes. This is not to suggest that there is anything 'illogical' in Hebraic thought, or in the gospel, but where we use the 'tools' of Greek philosophy to settle what Scripture means, we often end up by undermining Scriptural truths.

It is noteworthy that in the eighteenth century, during what historians call "The Enlightenment", Greek philosophy was reinvigorated in Western thought, and Greek philosophy once again became popular and dominant among the intelligentsia and ruling elites. The church once again became subject to these philosophical 'norms', and during this period there began two centuries of attack upon the truthfulness and dependability of Scripture. It is arguable that those attacks continue unabated in our own day.

The 'Greek mindset' is not the sole culprit in the church's weakened witness, but it is one area of church weakness that can be addressed by consciously seeking out a better and fuller understanding of the Hebraic dynamic underlying the Christian faith.

One New Man
This is the reality that believing-Jew and believing-Gentile are brought together as one before our Lord, through repentance (turning away from known sin) and placing our faith in Yeshua (Jesus). So we can declare along with Paul **There is neither Jew nor Greek, slave nor free, male nor female, for you are all one in Christ Jesus** (Galatians 3:28). This is what it means to be One New Man. This is the outcome of the New Covenant which grows out of the Old Covenant; the blessings of God's promises are extended

to all believers and are no longer experienced by trying to observe the Law; they are experienced only by faith in Yeshua (Jesus).

Jewish people still need to receive their Messiah. Jewish people do not need to become *culturally* 'Christian' (whatever that may mean – and the definitions of Christianity are numerous and confusing, as this book has sought to demonstrate!) but they, as all people everywhere, do need to become believers, to repent, be baptized and to be discipled by Yeshua (Jesus). Yeshua is the Saviour of Jews as much as He is of Gentiles. The consequences of rejection of Yeshua are the same for Jew as for Gentile.

I'm interested! What should I do next?

If you are not yet a Disciple of Jesus and want to know want it truly means to be His follower, then *now* is the best time to receive Him as Lord and as Saviour. You may want to talk to a trusted Christian friend who should be able to help you if you have some unanswered questions. If you are an established Christian/believer but sense that there is something missing in your walk with the Lord, and that exploring the Hebrew dynamic could be a key to growing deeper into Jesus, then look out some of the better books that should help to set some of the ideas explored in this book in a more concrete way.

20-20 Vision
Where there is no vision, the people perish (Proverbs 29:18).
If the trumpet does not sound a clear call, who will get ready for the battle? (1 Corinthians 14:8).
A sad sub-text to this book in each chapter has been the prospect of a time yet to come, but possibly now imminent, when the church will be in outright and bare-faced rebellion against the Lord. Some individual Christians will be in

rebellion, to be sure, simply in their laziness and worldliness rather than in their pursuit of their Lord. It is not so much that they are going out and committing 'the seven deadly sins', as it were, they are simply so engrossed in this world and so comfortable with it, so friendly towards it, that they allow their first love to die, they grow cold and wither. Change is imperceptible at first, and then one day there comes a time when they acknowledge they are no longer believers. We are reminded of householders who failed to see the thief coming (Matthew 24:43), and of wedding guests unprepared for their invitation (Matthew 22:8), and yet again of foolish maidens with insufficient oil in their lamps, and so missing the wedding feast (Matthew 25:12). Dear reader, I might ask you, as I must ask myself, how will you avoid this snare? Just what sort of believer are you? This is a question that each one of us needs to ask ourselves continually.

As you have reached this part of the book then hopefully you will by now share the author's overriding concern about the 'rebel church', hell-bent on defying the clear ordinances of God set out, for example, in the Ten Commandments. A few weeks before this book was begun, the Church of England was asked to contribute to the public debate shortly before the government changed the nature of marriage in the UK forever. The then new archbishop of Canterbury Justin Welby, said to be an 'evangelical', kept his head down in the run up to the final debates in the Houses of Commons and Lords in the UK parliament. The absence of his voice as head of the established church, and his silence in this matter, was deafening in the early part of 2013! No clarion trumpet call from the Archbishop. When he did finally pluck up the courage to speak, was there a clear and purposeful trumpet blast to rally the nation? Or even to rally the church? Welby made two comments in the Lords debate on 5 June 2013 that made it clear he was continuing to sit on the proverbial fence, as he had done all through the early part of that year. Firstly, he equated the new idea of homosexual marriage with God's call for a one-flesh relationship between man and woman. "It is clearly essential," said the Archbishop, "that stable and faithful same sex relationships should, where those involved want it, be recognised and supported with as much dignity and the same legal effect as marriage." It would be difficult in practice to interpret this as anything other than an agreement with the government's policy. The Archbishop was not arguing the principle, merely the details of implementation.

In acknowledging that the issue before the Lords was 'divisive', Welby expressed gratitude for the intervention of the Bishop of Salisbury (Nicholas Holtam), a well-known liberal. Perhaps Welby thought he needed to be seen to be even-handed in his attempt to hold together various turbulent priests within the desperately polarised Church of England. Welby was apparently determined not to be perceived as a turbulent priest! He accordingly referred to the "strong and welcome contribution" of Holtam. So what precisely had Holtam said? This was a reference to the widely publicised open letter of Holtam to Lord Ali, a 'gay Muslim' in which Holtam referred negatively to the Bible's witness as regards homosexual marriage in this way:

"The desire for the public acknowledgement and support of stable, faithful, adult, loving same sex sexual relationships *is not addressed by the six Biblical passages about homosexuality* which are concerned with sexual immorality, promiscuity, idolatry, exploitation and abuse. The theological debate is properly located in the Biblical accounts of marriage, which is why so many Christians see marriage as essentially heterosexual. However, *Christian morality comes from the mix of Bible, Christian tradition and our reasoned experience*. Sometimes Christians have had to rethink the priorities of the Gospel in the light of experience. For example, before Wilberforce, *Christians saw slavery as Biblical and part of the God-*

given ordering of creation. Similarly in South Africa the **Dutch Reformed Church supported Apartheid because it was Biblical and part of the God-given order of creation.** No one now supports either slavery or Apartheid. The Biblical texts have not changed; our interpretation has." *(Salisbury to Ali, June 2013 – emphasis by this author).*

If nothing else, in the context of this book we see in the above a clear dose of Greek thinking and a heavy use of eisegesis. The reference to a 'mix' of Bible, 'tradition' and 'reasoned experience' was pure Plato! The texts of the Bible were not to be taken at face value according to Holtam, they were to be re-thought and re-interpreted in the light of current social mores. The reference by Holtam to slavery and apartheid was a gross misrepresentation of what the Bible actually says. The Bible is strongly against slavery wherever it is mentioned. And apartheid is not mentioned at all. The fact that people may have eisegeted the Bible in the past to make it mean what they wanted it to mean was no justification for Holtam's commentary.

So the Bishop of Salisbury had denigrated the Bible before the nation, accusing it of supporting slavery and supporting apartheid. The nation at large could now perhaps be justified in side-lining the Word of God. And the Archbishop of Canterbury had lauded this misrepresentation as a "strong and welcome" contribution. We can see, then, that at the time of writing this book, church rebellion had reached all sections of the church – and whilst the C of E was perhaps no worse than some of the other 'denominations', it was supposed to be the established church and in that sense the 'first amongst equals'. In June 2013 there was a strong suspicion that the Church of England was more concerned about maintaining its privileged position as the 'established' church, and its various seats in the House of Lords. A vain hope in practice, as all the main political parties had by then expressed the desire to reduce (or eliminate) the church's footprint in the corridors of power. Rather than go out with a bang, the established church went out with a whimper. Less than four weeks after the marriage debacle, Justin Welby finally issued a clarion call to the nation as he took on the evil forces of a company called 'Wonga' a payday lender that charged exorbitant interest rates, a stance that Welby presumably thought would enable the Church of England to scale the moral heights once again. Welby said he wanted the C of E to use its considerable property portfolio to facilitate the establishment of local 'credit unions' and that he wanted to drive Wonga out of business. Within 24 hours he was having to explain the fact that the C of E was also an investor in Wonga.

Where does all this leave the individual believer, and that flock listening intently for their Shepherd's voice? By the middle of 2013 in the UK it was quite clear that the institutional/denominational church would stand firm on no issue of biblical substance. With frightened and possibly self-seeking 'shepherds' leading these churches there was a growing resignation amongst much of the flock of several denominations. Where will the church be by the year AD 2020? Eye specialists in the medical profession speak of 20-20 vision as being a measure of normal good vision and therefore of people who can see correctly and in that sense know where they are going! Jesus spoke of the blind leading the blind (Matthew 15:14). He was referring to the Pharisees in fact, but the phrase has widely come to represent all forms of rebellious leadership. And are at least some of our modern church leaders in fact 'Pharisaical' in their abandonment of people in their sins? Where the Pharisees of old heaped religious burden upon burden onto the people in their charge, modern clerics seem to do the opposite – to remove even what minimal moral constraints remain, and instead tell people their sins no longer matter because 'God understands their situation' and that 'God loves sinners'. Ergo, no need to repent as God loves me all the same! These church leaders do, in fact, in the words of the apostle Paul, give people precisely the message that their itching ears are eager to hear!

The individual believer, then, may have some un-comfortable choices to make. But one way to prepare for what lies ahead may be, as suggested above, to detox from Greek thinking and to try to emulate the mindset of our Lord. And the best phrase currently used to describe this is to adopt a 'Hebraic mindset'. In Appendix 2 we set out a 20-20 vision. This is the author's understanding of what true Christians need to do to prepare themselves to survive either within, or if necessary outside of, a thoroughly debased and rebellious church – a 'church' that seems now to be not so far away. There will in the immediate future, be three key currents in the so-called *sea of faith* that will facilitate and be emblematic of the final drift of the church away from its core mission – the clarion promotion of the gospel massage: **syncretism** – the melding of Christianity with the religions; **sexual licence** – the final abandonment of any biblical understanding of God's commands for one flesh relationships; **euthanasia** – the killing of sick people on the basis that it is 'kinder' to end their suffering.

Individual believers, then, need to challenge and to prepare themselves if they are to survive the storms ahead. The 20-20 vision set out in Appendix 2 is a good place to start. It is suggested that this is adopted as a faithful believer's personal Christian motif in the years ahead. Seven clear strands within this 'vision' should, taken together, help to strengthen us as we approach the year 2020. But of course this vision will still pertain beyond that year! This vision statement is offered as a helpful 'contract' that the believer can enter into with ... themselves! The Spirit will help you in this if you ask Him (so please do!). Your local church sadly may not help you in this, so at the end of the day this must be your decision and your responsibility. And that is why I call this a *contract with yourself.* Of course you do not have to do this alone, and indeed it would be best if you are able to connect with other concerned believers so you can uphold each other in prayer and in fellowship. Please turn now to Appendix 2 and prayerfully and seriously consider those seven core visions and what they mean to you. There are more subjects in this 20-20 vision statement than we have covered in detail in this book. We have not, for example, looked in detail at the plight of our suffering brothers and sisters in situations of persecution, yet their plight and our response to that plight absolutely has to be a part of our vision for the future. We have not looked at the scandalous nature of the gospel (surely the subject for a separate book) and yet an acknowledgement of that gospel message and its unacceptability to a world in sinful rebellion is something we do have to get to grips with.

So what is the bottom line in this? What precisely is being suggested by Appendix 2? The vision statement is set out in terms of what a faithful believer will be doing as part of their worship of God in the year 2020 (and beyond). These then will become the hallmarks of a believer who loves their Lord and wants to draw ever closer to Him. This will certainly change ourselves as individuals for the better, and indirectly will change the remnant church for the better. But most important, it will refresh our wonder at the gospel message and equip us to share it more clearly and more courageously with this world in desperate need.

"Happy are those who have been invited to the wedding feast of the Lamb"

Chapter Eight

THE PRODIGAL CHURCH

Of roots and rootedness (2)

I was once asked by a publisher to review an author's manuscript of a book examining 'Jewish Roots' and what these might mean for the church. As someone who was then relatively new to this area I immediately asked some trusted Christian friends to give me their speedy verdicts. The book alluded to the history of the Jewish people and the Jewish feasts. It pointed out, quite correctly, that some feasts are commanded by God, and others are purely cultural but deeply ingrained in the Jewish culture and mindset. I made a few suggestions to the author who seemed to receive them gratefully but there remained an element of doubt: whilst the writer specifically denied it, yet his book still seemed to be telling Christians to observe some, if not all, of the Jewish feasts. One of my friends wrote me a long and detailed review and ended this with the insightful comment: 'We do not put right 2000 years of Christian error by adopting 2000 years of Jewish error.' And my friend was a Christian well disposed to the need for a Hebraic insight to act as a corrective to so much that has been wrong in the church for so many centuries!

In our previous chapter we explored a little of what a greater Hebraic insight might give to individual Christians and what the concept of *one new man* means in practice. It is hoped that this introduction will help believers who are rightly concerned by the present trajectory of a broader institutional church that seems increasingly rebellious against the clear teaching of scripture and the basic traditions of the Christian faith. Straight away, however, we must sound some warning blasts. First, there is considerable resistance in the churches to the Hebraic Root and any study of it. The fears of the church hierarchies seem to include a loss of control and a fear of undermining of their own authority and their way of understanding and presenting the Bible. I will repeat something stated in the previous chapter. There remains a great deal of latent anti-Jewish feeling within the church, and the objection of church hierarchies to things Hebraic may well have this at the root. I apologise for being blunt. It is perhaps ironic that churches frequently flirting with syncretism and demanding a greater 'understanding' and 'respect for' other world faiths, will balk at exploration of the Hebraic root of Christianity! The one external relationship that matters fundamentally to Christianity and the one that has an end-time resonance is the one that must be kept off-limits!

A second element of resistance is not so negative. In fact it is in some respects quite positive and it is an objection which this author actually shares! It is simply this: there is a great deal of wacky theology out there that masquerades under the title 'Hebraic', and this confuses and upsets. It is upon this which we must now focus for a moment. Why is there confused teaching in this area? Why does it attract sometimes rather extreme 'interpretations'?

I offer just two thoughts. Readers will have to make up their own minds:

- The devil is active in this area. He must know that the reconciliation that is represented by *one new man* implies the devil's own death knell. It is in the devil's interests to keep Christians off-balance in this one area above all others! When believing Jew and believing

Gentile are reconciled, the end is nigh and the game is up – for the devil!

- The devil's favourite tactic is to counterfeit the truth. By mixing truth with error he can prevent the achievement of holiness within the Christian body corporate. At its most prosaic, we can say that by mixing truth with obvious error or wacky interpretations the devil can cast Hebraic understanding in a bad light and so keep Christians away from it.

We are warned by the apostle Paul not to be thrown about by sudden surges of new doctrine that emerge from time to time. The first major heresy to upset the early church was that of Gnosticism, and since then there have been innumerable ungodly teachings and heresies. Your author suggests that the church's widespread flirtation with 'the religions' (in particular Islam, Buddhism and Hinduism) is just such a surge in our own day. Paul speaks about believers growing into maturity and reaching 'unity' in the faith and in the knowledge of the Son of God. When this happens, says Paul, then **we will no longer be infants, tossed back and forth by the waves, and blown here and there by every wind of teaching and by the cunning and craftiness of men** (Ephesians 4:13–14). The word 'teaching' in the NIV is perhaps better rendered 'doctrine', as by the King James Version. From time to time such powerful 'waves' do indeed buffet the church, and they can confuse even the mature.[1] And, of course, what did Paul warn of in 2 Timothy 4:3? That people will one day 'not put up with sound doctrine'

---

[1] Notice in Ephesians 4:13–14 the combination of the waves of false teaching that, in a spiritual sense, 'knock us off our feet' with the cunning and craftiness of men. Your author predicts that by the third decade of the 21st century, with the craftiness of men persuading society and social mores that 'love' is the only litmus test that should govern our sexual behaviour, so then it will be widely taught and accepted that sexual purity is not a foundational aspect of Christian living. And so the church will adopt society's social mores in this area. We can see then, in practice, this unholy combination of false church teaching and the craftiness of men.

but instead will gather for themselves a **great number of teachers** to tell them what their 'itching ears' want to hear. Jesus warned of the same (Luke 21:8) when he said **watch out that you are not deceived**.

Paul went on, in his letter to the Colossian church, to encourage them (and us!) to be rooted in Jesus (Colossians 1:17) and so to be built-up in Him. Whilst there is so much that we can learn from the wonderful letter to the Colossian church, we should realise that Paul, who was himself a former rabbi, was writing to a church where Judaisers had been active and where they had managed to introduce false doctrine. This is why Paul makes his plea to individual believers: **see to it that no-one takes you captive through hollow and deceptive philosophy, which depends on human tradition and the basic principles of this world rather than on Christ** (Colossians 2:8). And why should they do this? **For in Christ all the fullness of the Deity lives in bodily form, and you have been given fullness in Christ, who is the head over every power and authority. In him you were also circumcised, in the putting off of the sinful nature, not with a circumcision done by the hands of men but with the circumcision done by Christ** (Colossians 2:9–11). Our relationship begins and ends in Christ, and there is absolutely no requirement to become Jewish or even to emulate Jewish people or their practices.

Now we know that Paul greatly valued his Jewish heritage (Acts 21:39; 20:16; 16:3; 1 Corinthians 9:20) and he explained the value of being a Jew (Romans 3:1–2). So there was nothing negative towards the Jews in Paul's strong warnings. Where Romans chapter 11 speaks of God's ongoing purposes for the Hebrew people, so Galatians chapters 4 and 5 specifically tell Gentile believers they are not to become Jewish. Some believers appear to have assumed that this was a way of reaching an exalted spiritual status. Plainly someone was spreading such a teaching.

The phrase 'Jewish roots' is not found in the Bible, so

we need to be careful about using it. Wherever there is an allusion to the Hebraic root, it is always singular (root) not plural (roots). When some Christians speak of *getting back to Torah*, they are perhaps unaware that there are several meanings to the term, none of which is particularly helpful to the normative Christian. By 'Torah' do people mean getting back to the whole Word of God (which would be a good thing)? Or do they just mean the first five books of the Bible – the books of Moses? (And if they mean this then what value do they place on all the rest of the books in the Bible?). If by Torah we are referencing the entire Old Testament, then does this somehow make the New Testament of less worth? Finally, if by Torah we mean what many modern Jewish people understand by the term (the books of Moses plus the oral law allegedly given to Moses at Sinai, plus rabbinic commentaries on the whole) then we are well adrift from normative Christianity.

The Hebraic root is best defined in the way that the apostle Paul did in Romans 11:18, where the apostle speaks three times of the high value of this root (singular). Where people speak unguardedly in Christian circles of the 'Jewish Roots Movement' or 'Hebraic Roots Movement' (plural) they may betray the provenance of the philosophy in their choice of the word 'Movement' which speaks more of a political movement for change rather than a work of the Holy Spirit. In other words, they are looking to man's strivings rather than God's anointing and enabling. None of this is to denigrate the important and legitimate desire to reconnect with Hebraic things, for they do have great value, as we began to explore in chapter 7. But we need to tread very carefully, and scripturally, and in step with the clear leading of the Holy Spirit. We should also be somewhat wary when some who expound this 'movement' begin to apply a mixture of Christian and Rabbinic thought, all held up as commendable. And all this in spite of the fact that in Colossians 2:8 Paul warns **see to it that no one takes you**

captive through hollow and deceptive philosophy, which depends on human tradition and the basic principles of this world rather than on Christ.

The letter is not specific about which heresies Paul had in mind as he wrote. Gnosticism is one likely candidate, but the reference to *not being judged* as regards food and drink or in respect of new moon festivals or Sabbath days suggests that some Judaising influence was also in Paul's thinking. It is ironic perhaps in the context of this book on the rebel church, where we have many times pointed out the dangers of Greek philosophy and the bad effect this has had on the history of the over-arching Christian church, to point out that there are Jewish philosophies of which the true Christian must also be wary.

Romans chapter 14 makes it reasonably clear that Jews are free to observe biblical Jewish customs if they choose to do so, but they should understand there is no spiritual merit within those customs, except insofar as they point towards Jesus (14:6). If the Old Testament laws are to be kept, it is to be voluntary. A legalistic approach to this merely brings people back under the yoke of the Law. It is to be repeated and emphasised, whilst a reconnection with our Jewish hinterland is commendable, we must tread carefully, and it is from the root (singular) that we should draw 'sap' and not from 'roots' which may be 'all over the place' in terms of philosophy. There can sometimes be a fine dividing line between truth and error.

Ultimately this battle is about the Word of God. That some Gentile believers of the apostolic church had developed feelings of superiority over their Jewish brethren, there can be little doubt. Paul found it necessary to slap them down over their pride (Romans 11:18–21). As Gentile believers we should have a sense of indebtedness to those whom God chose (and has now temporarily excluded) because we Gentiles have derived so many blessings and benefits from them. Their Messiah is our Lord. And God continues to work out His purposes through them. If the rebel church needs to return to anything, it is to the 'Jesus' root (or perhaps we should say the 'Yeshua' root) to which we should first turn. But, when all is said and done, a greater appreciation of and allegiance to our Hebraic root can only be of blessing to believers facing an uncertain future within (or perhaps increasingly outside of) a rebellious and debased church.

The prodigal church

If in this book there has been one villain seemingly in every chapter, it may perhaps have been seen as that hermeneutic called eisegesis (as opposed to exegesis) through which all too many theologians and clerics twist scripture to 'deliver' whatever spiritual 'lesson' they desire. I continue to believe that eisegesis is a dangerous hermeneutic but I will concede that it can be used by God, in spite of some of my earlier criticisms. It is quite possible that in individual circumstances an individual person might see a 'meaning' in a passage that speaks directly into their specific personal situation and which is not the primary purpose of the text. People do occasionally say they have received a specific answer to a problem in this way. That would be to eisegete (read into) a meaning or a purpose that the original biblical writer did not intend but which God can still make relevant in the *here and now*. The clear caveat on this must be that Scripture must be used to interpret Scripture. So an eisegeted 'meaning' could never run counter to, or contradict, the clear revelation of Scripture – as sometimes, for example, so-called Christians will say they believe that a Bible verse told them to divorce their spouse and re-marry because they now 'love' another and, well, God is love! So I would still caution that eisegesis honoured by God is in fact quite rare. We are far more likely to find direct answers to life's problems by reading out of (exegeting) the clear witness of the Bible.

But I hope readers will bear with me for a moment whilst I break my own rule! The parable of the prodigal son (Luke

15:11–32) speaks first and foremost of the *agape* (love) of God in forgiving even direct and wilful sin once that essential precondition of repentance has been met. That is the plain primary reason for the parable and, following directly in Luke's gospel, those parables of the lost sheep, and the lost coin, so it is easy to see how this parable of the lost son 'fits in' with the Lord Jesus' broader theme about forgiveness and restoration – of being 'lost' and then 'found'. The unforgivingness of the older brother is always a puzzling postscript to the parable. We tend to wonder why the parable seems to leave the story with what might seem an ambiguous or unhappy end. (The answer to that, of course, is that the parables of Jesus always tell us the truth, and are not merely given to provide happy endings for our pleasure!) Some commentators refer to the parable as *the parable of the lost sons* (plural), noting that both sons were unloving to their father, and that he forgave them both. But I believe we can legitimately read into this parable an additional sub-text: this would be the idea that the two sons represent Messianic Jews and the Gentile church. By this way of reasoning, the younger son becomes the Jewish nation who so bitterly rebelled against the Father and as a result spent years in the wilderness – far away from home. But eventually a change of heart happened and the younger son (Jewish believers) repent and return. Are they then welcomed with open arms by the older brother (the Gentile church)? You know the answer!

I am well aware that this eisegesis, this reading-in a 'meaning' that is not obviously there, fails at one crucial point. It might be objected that the Hebrew believers would 'naturally' be the older brother and the Gentile church the younger, because the gospel was first given to the Hebrews and only later to those newcomers – the Gentiles. Well, perhaps. But could it also be argued that, in a sense, the Gentile church has become the older brother in the key reality of now vastly outnumbering the Jewish believing community, and having (for better or for worse) developed and evolved the "Christian religion" for the past two thousand years? And in that sense can we legitimately argue that the roles are reversed? Allowing that this could be the case, how then does the parable play out? We now see the younger son as the one who has rebelled and who has as a consequence been exiled (self-exiled in the terms of the parable). After rejecting Jesus and as a direct result, there does seem to have been a clear 'judgement' on the Hebrew Nation as a nation, and for the better part of two thousand years the Hebrew people were exiled in large part, from the Promised Land. The older son in the parable had worked tirelessly for his father in the intervening years – but like the younger son his heart, too, was far away. He sullenly worked at the family business in the hope of inheriting all, only to find that his wayward brother returned and their father rejoices in this return. In some way there must now be a major adjustment in the relationships. The story did not play out in the way the older brother had assumed. The rebellious younger son has been welcomed back not as a servant (the role the elder brother assumed the younger would get). No, he is reinstated as a son. So the older brother *will* have to make some major accommodation for the younger, whether he likes it or not.

Could this be the Gentile church? Angrily disappointed that there are Jewish believers in Jesus lately welcomed back into the fold and saying, accusingly, to the Father **"all these years I have worked for you like a slave, and I have never disobeyed your orders. What have you given me?"** (Luke 15:29, GNB). It almost begins to look as though the 'hard work' of the older son was not so much for love, but for reward. And when the Gentile church discovers that the reward must be shared with the rebellious 'younger' brother (those who only lately have come to faith in Yeshua [Jesus]) so, then, resentment builds, especially as this means that the sole authority of the 'elder' brother out in the fields, acting on behalf of the father, is now drawing to a rapid close.

The parable of the prodigal son does not demonstrate conclusively that the older son *had* in fact obeyed his father
without fault. That was his self-assessment, not necessarily
his father's assessment. His father politely does not argue the
point in Luke 15. What he does say, however, is intriguing
(v. 31): **"My son. You are always here with me, and
everything I have is yours."** This could well speak to the
church – to those Gentile believers grafted in to the olive
tree that is Israel and drawing strength and nourishment
from that Hebraic root. *Everything God gives is given to
us without demur.* Whatever was given to the Hebrews by
way of covenantal promises is extended to Gentile believers.
"Everything I have is yours." We are adopted into His
family. We are in-grafted as wild branches into the Hebraic
root. But, God has made it plain that at a certain point in
history, a full sufficiency[2] of Gentiles would be brought in
to God's family, and then the Jewish nation would in large
part turn to Yeshua (Jesus), thus fulfilling God's purposes
for this world prior to the second coming of Jesus.

I repeat, this reading-in to the *parable of the prodigal son*
a meaning that *may* not be there must be problematic. And
yet the touch-points with the wider witness of scripture are
startling: the old covenant was always going to be expanded
and reconfigured by a new covenant. God's broader purpose
in choosing the Hebrew nation as His special possession
was always, through them, to reach out to all mankind. But
what of the reaction of the church, this 'older' brother that
we have identified? Even with the assurance that everything
of the father's is *also their possession*, do they rejoice
at the return of the younger? No, they do not, generally
speaking. The church seems at best ambivalent to the idea
of Messianic believers, and at worst outright dismissive. The
old established churches seem embarrassed when Messianic
believers are in discussion. They would much rather 'deal
with' rabbinic Jews, especially when reaching out to the

---

[2] Romans 11:25(b)

Jewish community, than to those Jews who have placed their faith in Yeshua (Jesus). These people do not 'fit' the template, and challenge the church's understanding of itself. And as we have observed elsewhere, the church in our own day is growing in its hostility towards Israel, siding ever more openly with one political faction in the Middle East, and openly disputing the possibility that God would return the Jewish people to the land He had set aside for them. And did not Jesus Himself say that, as regards those lands, that the times of the Gentiles would be "fulfilled" (Luke 21:24)? In other words *the times of the Gentiles* would end at some point.

Why is the 'mainstream' church so antipathetic towards Israel? The established church dislikes Jews. Of that there can be little real doubt. It will deny it with every breath, but, as is often said, actions speak louder than words. Certainly the so-called liberal church does actively dislike Israel, and increasingly the 'evangelical' (especially Anglican evangelical) church takes the same view. But what is the *real* underlying reason? Could it really be that, like the older brother in the parable, the presence of the Hebrew people in Israel spells the imminent end of the church's hegemony over the gospel, as these believing Jews also share the good news of Yeshua with the wider world? And could it be that the very idea of the possible physical return of Jesus in glory, which the precursor return of the Hebrew nation to Israel presages, be something that the established churches would resent and resist? I would only say, in conclusion, that the rebel church (and very often this means the established/ denominational churches) will become increasingly bold and vocal against Israel, and dismissive towards those Jews who know Yeshua (Jesus) as Lord and as Saviour, in the years ahead. Watch this space!

The Gospel and the Church

It is surprisingly difficult to summarise what the good news (or gospel) actually is, in the sense of speaking definitively and with absolute precision. Why do we need to look at 'the gospel' in detail in this book about the rebel church? We need to look at it for two principal reasons: (1) there is evidence that some churches offering to the world a watered-down, user-friendly 'gospel' which helps to mask their own rebellion; and (2) there may be some confusion in the minds of our own readers as to precisely what the good news is! Now, dear reader, I will ask you, if you are a church-attending Christian, if you can now summarise to yourself, perhaps using a key verse from the Bible, what is the gospel. You might want to pause just now for a moment to consider this. If there is one Bible verse above all others that is likely to spring to mind, you might name it now – book, chapter and verse! If there is such a single 'gospel in a nutshell' then many would consider it to be John 3:16. Is this, however, the gospel? David Pawson argues powerfully in two short books that it is not (*Is John 3:16 the Gospel?* and *The God and the Gospel of Righteousness*, both published by Terra Nova Publications, 2008, still widely available at the time of writing this book, and both used as inspiration in the following section). The gospel is often presented along these lines: *God loves you, has a wonderful plan for your life, and will accept you if you in turn accept Jesus.* Some churches do not even go that far! Some now teach that God accepts you whoever you are, whatever you have done and in whatever state you finally leave this world! This is called 'universalism' and runs along the lines 'God is so loving even Hitler[3] will be saved!' But is this what Jesus taught?

There seem to be three gospel schemes in wide circulation and we will summarise them in prosaic form, so I apologise

[3] For those who do not know, Adolf Hitler was the German dictator who began the Second World War in 1939 – a war that cost some thirty million people their lives in Europe

in advance to my readers for what may be considered great imprecision! However you will hopefully quickly see the point of this and how this chimes with our theme of the rebel church. What then is *the good news*? Is it simply that God loves you? If your answer is yes then the 'gospel' goes something like this (scheme A)

- I was born a scoundrel
- I lived the life of a scoundrel
- I died a scoundrel
- But that's all right because God loves me!

This is perhaps the idea of universalism. It evolves into a philosophy that makes "god" a sort of easygoing grandfather-in-the-sky deity who is not fussed about your religion (as 'he' owns them all!) and will 'save' everyone through Jesus. Does your church teach this 'gospel'? The above might be modified slightly in this way (scheme B):

- I was born a scoundrel
- I lived the life of a scoundrel
- I became a Christian so then I led a somewhat better life
- I died not as bad as I began!
- But that's all right because God loves me!

Is this all there is to it? To attend at least some churches we could be excused for thinking it is. The only verse every Christian is pretty much guaranteed to know off by heart, as we have seen, is John 3:16, but many consider this verse has been taken out of context and is mis-applied. More traditional churches might render the gospel in this way (scheme C):

- I was born a scoundrel
- I lived the life of a scoundrel
- I met Jesus and received Him into my life [Justification] and Jesus progressively made me more like Him
- My subsequent life was one of joy and service [Sanctification]
- God receives me because Jesus died in my place.

Scheme C is closer to the biblical ideal, to be sure. But it is still highly transactional in its approach and therefore seems to sell the good news short – and that in turn means to sell Jesus short. In scheme C we included two technical theological words [in brackets] which helpfully describe the process with a little more precision. Indeed scheme C acknowledges salvation as being a journey, rather than as an event. It is writer Mike Endicott who helpfully speaks of *the gate of justification* leading on to *the road to sanctification* (see Further Reading – *Kingdom Seekers*). Even in scheme C as we have colloquially summarised it, we have not really identified just what it is that God graciously offers, and of which we as individuals have the option to accept, or reject. If there is a key and un-bridgeable distinction between biblical Christianity and *the religions* (e.g. Islam, Buddism, Hinduism, Judaism etc) it must be this: Christianity is in one sense highly individualistic – though perhaps 'personal' would be a better term for believers are brought into fellowship with all other true Christians – in the sense that God offers an opportunity which at an individual level you either accept or reject (and rejection does not have to be a positive thing – it can also be quite simply in ignoring the wonderful offer that has been made – ignoring the cross of crucifixion). Jesus spoke of repenting, and about *believing in Him* (or believing *on* Him), which includes *trusting Him*. (It is more than believing things *about* Him, though it includes that too.) Jesus also speaks of being *born of water and the Spirit*. So Christians speak of 'new birth', which should be the beginning of a walk of obedience to Jesus, relying on His Word and the Holy Spirit for living life, having been made a 'new creation'.

So God deals with us as persons. Non-Christian 'religions', by contrast, see an individual as being born into their religion, from which they may not escape (except, in some cases, at the risk of rejection and death). The individual is subsumed into their community and is not known by their god as distinct – hence the Islamic concept of the 'umma' for example – that community of followers of Allah – where the community assumes responsibility for the individual. And hence no individual relationship of child to parent can be experienced. No Muslim or Hindu could ever call God 'Abba' as can a believer in Jesus (Galatians 4:6–7).

It is fair to say that God was never addressed in prayer as 'Father' until Jesus came to earth and revealed Him in this way. In His prayer to His Father, Jesus said, "**I have made you** [your name] **known to them, and will continue to make you known in order that the love that you have for me may be in them and that I myself may be in them**" (John 17:26). To what name was Jesus referring? It was the name 'Father'. If there is anything close to Jesus' heart, it is to introduce God as 'Father' to us. Elsewhere Jesus said, **"do not worry, saying, 'What shall we eat?' or 'What shall we drink?' or 'What shall we wear?' For your heavenly Father knows that you need them"** (Matthew 6:31–32). In addition, He said, **"If you then, being evil, know how to give good gifts to your children, how much more will your Father who is in heaven give good things to those who ask Him!"** (Matthew 7:11).

We can say emphatically, then, that to know God through Jesus is to know Him as Father.

Perhaps a more accurate way of thinking about the gospel message than is highlighted in our schemes A, B and C above, is to express this divine transaction (Jesus taking our punishment on Himself) more in terms of what is given to the believer as well as what is taken away from him, or from her. The flaw in the above schemes, even scheme C, is that they do not go far enough! Even with justification sorted out, and with the journey of sanctification safely embarked upon, if you were to die tonight – and indeed if I were to die tonight – why on earth should God have you or me, anywhere near Him? We know from Jesus that only people who are completely right before God will be with Him for eternity (Revelation 21:27). I know I am not completely right before God – and if I may risk offending my readers, I know that you are not completely right either! We will never be completely right in this life, so we can never enter that place where absolutely everything is right, because if we did, then we would simply pollute it. We would spoil it. It would no longer be holy. So what is the remedy? How is this eternal conundrum finally and permanently resolved? Plainly it is not by keeping God's holy laws, because we cannot do it, we are simply incapable of doing it. God's chosen people (the Hebrews) were given God's laws and the responsibility to live them as a sort of spiritual prototype on behalf of all mankind, blazing a trail of obedience that the rest of humanity might follow! The Hebrews failed, just as any other nation would have failed. That is why God always had in mind the new and better covenant, inaugurated by the blood of Jesus Christ Himself.[4]

What is this better alternative, this good news? What does Christianity offer that 'the religions' cannot? What does the gospel offer? We learn from the apostle Paul: **I am not ashamed of the gospel, because it is the power of God for the salvation of everyone who believes: first for the Jew, then for the Gentile. For in the gospel a *righteousness* from God is revealed, a *righteousness* that is by faith from first to last, just as it is written: "The *righteous* will live by faith** (Romans 1:16–17; emphasis by author). Three times here is the offer of righteousness. We can never make it on our own. We can never make ourselves righteous enough. But God offers us His righteousness. God is showing us that we will never have enough of our own, so instead the **gospel of God** (Romans 1:1) offered us the righteousness of Jesus Himself, given by grace (meaning: as undeserved gift), through faith in Jesus' crucifixion and resurrection. Reflecting the *gate of Justification* and the *highway of*

---

[4] The reader is referred to Hebrews chapters 8 and 9.

sanctification that we met earlier, we can say that God's righteousness is **imputed** to us when we are born again – when we receive Jesus as our Lord and Saviour, and God's righteousness is **imparted** to us progressively as we go through life – and that is imparted righteousness. So, we are first saved, as we are justified by faith (and we are justified by the judge – God) as we go through that gate of justification. We are justified – a legal term – and Christ's righteousness is *imputed* to us. Then God's righteousness is *imparted* progressively to us as we walk that highway towards the cross. Remember what Jesus said: **narrow is the road that leads to life, and only a few find it** (Matthew 7:14). By faithfully treading that pathway, we become progressively more like our Saviour. That is *imparted* righteousness – from the Holy Spirit, imparted to the disciples of Jesus.

Righteousness is *imputed* through Jesus and *imparted* through the Holy Spirit. It is fairly said, that all three Persons in the Trinity are involved in this process of Salvation. Imputed righteousness represents and explains God's forgiveness of our past sinful life. If God were to forgive our sin without any conditions it would be unrighteous of Him to do so. And yet He pronounces us saints because of Jesus and what Jesus has achieved. There is no such thing as 'unconditional' forgiveness. It would be wrong for a good and righteous God to forgive sins unless two conditions were met. Firstly, *that our sins should have been paid for already* – which is what Jesus has done for us. The heart of the gospel is that Jesus has already paid. This is why there can be no forgiveness without the cross. We can say emphatically that every act of forgiveness is written in the blood of Jesus. That is what my forgiveness and your forgiveness actually cost. But there is a second condition: this condition is on our side. *We are to repent toward God.* Repentance is something we do – it includes a change of lifestyle, and is marked by contrition and a sense that we have not only offended against other people but against our Creator Himself.

So that is it! That is the divine transaction. It is not only that God loves you, although God's agape (love) is clearly crucial (literally) in giving His Son to die in our place, saving us from the penalty our sins deserved. The truly good news is also that Jesus will make you right, and so present you as righteous before His Father. Repentance is the first essential step to becoming a Christian, and this means turning away from, turning our back upon, our old life. It certainly means a change in lifestyle, perhaps getting out of wrong relationships, perhaps giving up on besetting sinful habits which are harmful to us or to others. The good news (or gospel) is an offer, not just of *forgiveness* (which is only the beginning) but also of *righteousness*. It is an offer to make bad people into good people, of turning sinners into saints. We revert, then, to the question of what sort of 'gospel' is your church preaching? What sort of 'gospel' do you believe in? A rebel church seems extremely comfortable with a 'gospel' of 'God's *unconditional* love'. Again, that adjective is never used in the Bible of His love! Read some of the conditions Jesus sets out in John chapter 14! True repentance and new birth is seldom taught in the rebel church. Perhaps, at the most, some minor adjustments to smooth away some of the more obvious of our 'selfish' misdemeanours, but that is about it!

The *true* gospel is a double exchange. We give to Jesus our sins and He gives to us His righteousness. Plainly this is an unequal exchange: in a very real sense it is we, as repentant sinners, who get the best part of the bargain. It does seem, however, that many people are very happy with the thought of the *forgiveness*, and thereby what they see as the guaranteed escape from the consequences of sin, but are far less comfortable with the *righteousness* which Jesus proffers in return – that REAL change in our lives. In fact some of us do not want to accept Jesus' righteousness at all. There is that old idea of: 'Please God, make me holy – but not just yet'! Perhaps it is true to say that many folk want to stop at half a gospel. Does your church help them to see this travesty of truth? What precisely does your church teach in this regard?

The Gospel Equation

Will a rebel church present a clear gospel message? Whilst this book has sought to identify rebel traits in today's church and to compare these with the clear warnings given by the Lord Jesus about the preparedness of His church for His return, there was an inevitability that we would review the gospel message, as any serious Christian book is likely to do at some point. The gospel lies at the heart of all we do. We said earlier that it can be quite difficult to summarise the gospel, and we have suggested that some attempts by the wider church to present a gospel message that is intelligible, actually succeed only in watering it down. Your author responded to a friend via e-mail over a few weeks early in 2013, when my friend asked for a dependable statement of what it means to be a Christian, reduced to just one sentence! A good challenge, and I struggled a little bit to develop one. But in the end we settled on a form of words we both agreed seemed to 'fit the bill'! As they say colloquially, if you want to find your prince, then you have to kiss a few frogs first! In the same way I prepared and then immediately eliminated some sentences that failed to 'fit the bill' adequately. Let's look at them before settling on my own favourite:

Being a Christian means to be first a disciple of Jesus, following in His footsteps and in His power, and second to be one who has made a conscious decision to follow Him as Lord (as in John 3:16)
This is part way there. It places the primacy of Jesus first and indicates being Jesus' disciple (linked to our word discipline). So we are seeing Jesus as our 'Master' and 'Lord'. But then I really need to add those things. This also hints at forgiveness, but again I have not said it.

Being a Christian means to BELIEVE in the efficacy of the cross
This is OK so far as it goes. It cites the cross and hints at forgiveness, but says nothing of NEW LIFE. So it won't do. It also speaks of the 'mechanics' of being 'saved' but nothing of the reason.

Being a Christian means having a relationship with the Godhead through Jesus the Son of God
Again good so far as it goes. It pulls out the RELATIONSHIP aspect, but again says nothing of new life, the Cross etc. So to that extent, it is inadequate.

Being a Christian means to be 'saved' from the power, effects and consequences of sin
Again there's some real truth in this, but WHY does God the Father save us through God the Son? Where is forgiveness – and where are the two commands that Jesus said were the MOST important i.e. to love God first (the Jewish 'Shema'), and to love one's neighbour as oneself?

So, in the fullness of e-mail exchanges, we settled on the definition below. But first with a necessary explanatory note (which my friend pointed out meant I had in reality failed to achieve a one-sentence definition!). Theologically speaking, a Christian is someone who has received the Jesus as Lord and Saviour (John 1:12), trusts Him alone for the forgiveness of sins (Acts 4:12), has put no trust in his own efforts (Isaiah 64:6) to please God, and has repented from his/her sins (Mark 1:15). So my final, one sentence working definition was this:

To be a Christian means to follow Christ, to desire Him, to fellowship with Him, to be indwelt by Him, and to bring glory to Him in your life

This definition I believe covers some of the deficiencies in the earlier attempts, if only by implication. A single sentence achieved, but assumes a certain background 'understanding', as in my explanatory note, above.

The week that this chapter was prepared, your author was also engaged in an e-mail conversation on Linked-In, via one of its Christian discussion groups. One contributor asked if there was a useful *gospel formula* that one could apply. It was perhaps the same sort of idea as my friend had – to reduce the gospel down to its essence in a reasonably intelligible way. As with the attempt at a one-sentence definition, this proved to be a difficult; but a helpful exercise, even so. Without being definitive (because in truth it is perhaps impossible to be definitive in such a simplistic way) the group early on hit upon this, as a useful starter:

Ephesians 2:8 – **"For by grace are ye saved through faith; and that not of yourselves: it is the gift of God**...."

Therefore: **Grace + Faith = Salvation**

Without Grace – no salvation

Without Faith – no salvation

Whilst this formula, *Grace + Faith = Salvation*, does not specifically draw out repentance, the cross and new birth, they are certainly implied in the above. Salvation, said one contributor, is *by* God's grace *through* faith. Its author added the following helpful clarifications:

* Grace MUST be God's definition of Grace...

* Faith MUST be in Christ's death (Cross), burial, and resurrection for our sins...

* The fact that Jesus had to die to PAY the PRICE for my sins MUST lead to my repentance!

In this equation, then, we see that Grace AND Faith are essential for Salvation. Many people proclaim salvation is by Grace, which is true. However, without the conduit of Faith, we do not receive the Grace.

We cannot close this discussion of our efforts to distil the heart of what the New Testament presents as the good news (gospel) without referring to Paul's summary. Elsewhere, he refers to other aspects, but this has to be the heart of the matter, and we note that unlike the teachings of all other religions, and unlike much that passes for a 'gospel' in the rebel church it consists of powerful proclamation of historic, living reality, embodying the key truth claim:

Now, brothers, I want to remind you of the gospel I preached to you and on which you have taken your stand. By this gospel you are saved if you hold firmly to the word I preached to you. Otherwise, you have believed in vain. For what I received I passed on to you as of first importance: that Christ died for our sins according to the Scriptures, that he was buried, that he was raised on the third day according to the Scriptures, and that he appeared to Peter and then to the Twelve. After that, he appeared to more than five hundred of the brothers at the same time, most of whom are still living, although some have fallen asleep.... (1 Corinthians 1ff.)

Paul's summary of the good news (quite a bit longer than than a sentence!) goes on to mention the appearances of the risen Lord Jesus to James and to himself.

What a glorious contrast that true gospel is, compared with all the false 'gospels', false religions and vacious syncretistic ideas devised by men. The authentic good news is so full of life and resurrection power – the real power of the living God which raised Jesus from the dead, changing lives. It was an offence to Greeks and and it is a stumbling block to Jews until they encounter and believe in the crucified and risen one who is alive and is Himself the Truth! The true gospel was given by God (see Romans 1:1) and is not a theological construct put together by a consensus of theologians!

This book draws to a rapid close. Enough has been said to warn individual Christians of the convulsions that lie ahead. Certainly more can be written on this subject (and no doubt will be!) but the wise and prudent Christian will heed the warnings that Jesus gave. Jesus asked a rhetorical question in Luke 18:8 that must cause us to stop and think: **when the Son of Man comes, will he find faith on the earth?** The book of Revelation indicates that when the Son returns, the broad, unsaved world will be in a situation of utmost rejection of the gospel. Perhaps we should say, this situation is 'a given'. It should not surprise us. It is the rebellion of the church that bears His Name that *should* surprise us. And yet Jesus has clearly predicted it. Some leaders will be in outright rebellion in a manner that must be called apostasy. The 'ordinary believers' (sometimes thought of as 'the laity') may in large measure be asleep, unaware of the impending disaster and their own unpreparedness to meet their Lord. We were reminded in Chapter 2 (Ready or Not, He is Coming) that Jesus spoke the parable of the 'Ten Virgins', sometimes called 'the wise and foolish virgins' (Matthew 25:1–13). Whether this parable is a precise mathematical statement about the unpreparedness of sections of the church – where five out of ten virgins are unable to attend the wedding feast because of their unpreparedness – we cannot really say. But the very thought that fifty per cent of Christians might be excluded from the wedding feast should be enough to make us sit up and take notice!

In the Introduction we looked at some huge question-marks that sit over at least some of the leadership of the traditional, and especially 'episcopal', types of church. Now this is not to be confused with the eccentric Episcopalian Church of the USA (which is part of the Anglican communion worldwide). By 'episcopal' we refer to those church structures governed through "bishops" and broadly this must include Roman, Orthodox and many Protestant churches – especially the 'established' churches. Lest any of the non-denominational churches are tempted to think that these problems of rebellion and false doctrines do not apply to them, we have only to remember that there are various abuses reported from time to time even with these churches. What does the Bible warn about church leaders? The Lord Himself spoke obliquely about church leaders – or false church leaders – when He referred to the blind leading the blind (Matthew 15:13–14; Luke 6:39–40). In Matthew 15 He was certainly speaking about the Pharisees, and challenging their leadership. But does He by the same token speak into our situations of at least some of today's church leaders? This must be a challenge to the individual Christian who is to listen intently for their Shepherd's voice (John 10:27). But it is even more a challenge to church leaders who too often seem to adopt the standards of this world. In James 3:1 the apostle speaks a truth of which every Christian needs to be aware: **Not many of you should presume to be teachers, my brothers, because you know that we who teach will be judged more strictly**. That is a stark warning to church leaders, to those shepherds who are supposed to protect the flock from external threats, and not to serve as agents to introduce those threats directly into the sheep fold. The leader has an additional responsibility before Jesus. But the individual Christian also has a responsibility before God. *We should not allow ourselves to be led by those who introduce false 'gospels' which progressively become less and less distinct from the world.* If your church's leadership is introducing, for example, the heresies of syncretism or sexual license, or preaching a social gospel, then it may be high time for you to find a new home.

We have not referenced the Old Testament very much in this book, but if there is one key theme that runs throughout those 39 books that make up the Old Testament, it is that God will preserve for Himself a faithful remnant, those who will not bow the knee to Baal, or whatever other 'god' the world demands we should worship. When Jesus returns, He will call to Himself 'the elect', those whose names were written in the Lamb's book of life from the beginning of time. We should not, therefore feel too down-hearted about the outright rebellion of the church against the clear revelation of Scripture. There will continue to be many who will actively seek Jesus until the end. And they will be on the winning side! But we do have to be on our guard, and the times we live in do seem to be portentous – *the calm, perhaps, before the storm*?

The good news for today is that the Bridegroom is coming at a specific point in time. Probably soon, in terms of world history. We must cleanse ourselves and be ready – keeping oil in our lamps, ready to be part of that wedding procession which Jesus will lead. Watch Israel – and watch what your church leaders teach about Israel. These do seem to be litmus tests of where people stand. Most of all, be faithful to Him, our Rock and our Salvation! And God willing, we will rejoice together at the great wedding feast!

"Happy are those who have been invited to the wedding feast of the Lamb" – Revelation 19:9

APPENDIX 1

See Chapter Five: *How the Church Lost the Way*

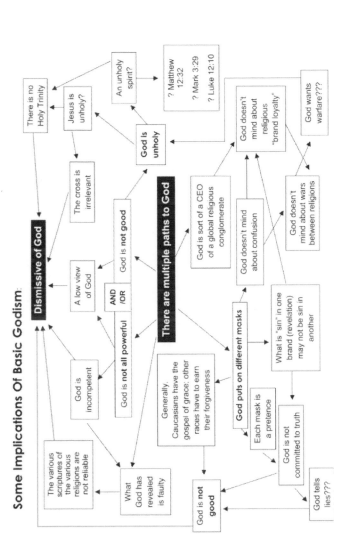

APPENDIX 2

20–20 Vision	*Changing the Church for the better.... Changing ourselves for the better....*		
Vision No.	Vision Description	Key Text	Commentary
1	Disciples of Jesus listening intently to the Shepherd's voice.	John 10:27	Today there are many siren voices which try to persuade us to take our eyes away from Jesus. But His disciples know His voice and feel deeply uncomfortable when a "gospel" is preached that is not totally focused on Jesus. The task of the true disciple of Jesus is to constantly listen out for His voice.
2	Disciples of Jesus attuned to the scandalous nature of the Gospel message – and sharing it joyously.	1 Cor 1:23	The gospel – the reality that it is ONLY through a crucified God that we may find ultimate peace – is a scandal to the world at large. Christians need to be attuned to the reality that this gospel is a scandal. Very often the world sees the gospel not as good news but as bad news!
3	Disciples of Jesus seeking to understand end-time realities whilst witnessing to a real-time world.	Acts 1:7–8	It is clear that God does have an end-time plan and we are called to be aware of "signs" that the end may be near. But in the meantime and for always, our call is to witness to Jesus to a now-time world.
4	Disciples of Jesus at ease with the reality of "one new man" – believing Jew and believing Gentile united in Christ.	Eph 2:15	It is clear that God continues to work out His purposes through the Hebrew people (Ephesians 2:11–22 and Romans chapters 9–11). Christians seem to react violently either becoming very anti-Jewish or very pro-Jewish. But the call is to understand - to recognise what God is doing and to wonder at the outworking of His covenantal purposes. That is why we need to be "at ease" with these concepts. Otherwise we will be perplexed!
5	Disciples of Jesus rejoicing in the Hebraic root, understanding Jesus in His Hebraic hinterland and rejoicing in the precisely balanced relationship of NT & OT.	Rom 11:11–12	Jesus came to bring the good news first to the Hebrews and then to the wider world (John 10:16). His family was always going to be enlarged. God's covenant with the nation of Israel was always going to be enlarged. The challenge for believers today is to understand God's ongoing purposes in the land He has set aside as His land for His people, as well as His purposes in the wider world.
6	Disciples of Jesus praying and working tirelessly for our persecuted brothers and sisters.	John 15:18–21	There has always been persecution and always will be. The Bible makes it clear that at the end persecution will entail significant analogies with persecution at the beginning. Whilst we have the freedom and ability to act, we owe a special debt to our suffering brothers and sisters, wherever they may be.
7	Disciples of Jesus commited to prayer and to the study of the Bible.	1 Thess 5:16–18	Prayer is always the believer's vital breath. If we do not pray, we will not see God's power displayed. God gives us the privilege of praying direct, not through priest or intermediary, but through Jesus our Lord (John 14:13). God has given us His word; it is the utmost folly for a believer not to read, mark, learn and inwardly digest the word He has given.

APPENDIX 2

Vision No.	Supplementary Texts
1	Psalm 23; John 10:1–30; Hebrews 2:1
2	Colossians 1:15–23
3	2 Peter 3; Revelation 22:7–17; 1 Thessalonians 4:13 – 5:11; 2 Thessalonians 2 ; 2 Timothy 3
4	Ephesians 2:11–22; Colossians 2:6–12; Romans 10:16–11:12
5	Romans 1:16; Matthew 15:24; 2 Timothy 3:16 (note – precisely what Scripture was Paul referring to?); Luke 24 – especially v. 27.
6	Matthew 5:3–12 (especially vv. 11–12); Matthew 10:17–42; Mark 13:9; John 15:18–16:4; Revelation 2:9–10 and 13; Revelation 6:9– 11; Romans 8:17; Ephesians 6:18
7	Matthew 6:9–13; Philippians 4:6–7; 1 John 5:14–15; Jeremiah 29:11–15; Matthew 21:21–22; Acts 2:42; Jeremiah 33:3; James 1:5–7

APPENDIX 3

A Covenant God

God is a promise-keeping God. He makes His covenants and we must respond to those covenants, either in faith or rejection.

Which covenants are still in force? The table on the next two pages suggests it is only the Moses covenant that has been replaced – and that it has been replaced by the Messianic covenant, which ushers in a new age.

Each covenant has been given a number for ease of reference. Each row in the table shows with whom the covenant was established, and its conditionality.

Note to Appendix 3

Does this matter? Is this just ancient history or dry theology? Many Christians hold that these truths speak into our situation today; in particular into the world in which we currently live, the growth of the Messianic Jewish movement and the restoration of the Jewish people to their biblical home land. Are these accidents of history, or is God working out his covenantal promises as He said He would? Finally, these texts help us to understand which covenants are timeless and therefore still apply. Crucially they suggest that it is the Moses covenant that has been 'replaced', by being extended and enlarged to cover all mankind. Today God appoints a royal priesthood of all those who are true disciples of Jesus.

	Made with	Key text	Commentary
0	Adam	Gen 2:16	We are free to live in peace and to enjoy all that God gives. We are not, however, free to sin without consequence. Whilst this is not truly a covenant, it is included in this list to give perspective to the other five covenants.
1	Noah	Gen 9:16	God in fact made an extended covenant with Noah, in terms of protecting Noah and his family. Gen 6:18; Gen 8:21b; Gen 9:3 (reminiscent of Gen 1:29); Gen 9:11 through 17.
2	Abraham	Gen 12:2-3	Repeated and emphasised: Gen 12:7; Gen 15:5-7; Gen 22:16-18; Ex 3:8, Ex 3:17; Ex 6:6-8
3	Moses	Ex 19:5-6	The Hebrews become a nation of priests: this is a blessing to the whole world. Ex 20 (all) and Ex 34:10ff set out the conditions applicable.
4	David	2 Sam 7:13-16	God promises to establish a house for Himself forever (2 Sam 7:13). This is a direct Messianic promise, as God works out His purpose to bless all Mankind. See 1 Sam 16:13. Also 2 Sam 7 (all) and 2 Sam 23:5.
5	Messianic		Having established His covenant with Israel through Abraham and promised a House through David, the covenantal promises now become more explicit, as God points towards what the Messianic office entails, how the Messianic line would bring life from death, and Who that Messiah would be - principally in terms of the suffering servant. God reveals these truths through three major prophets:
5A	Jeremiah (what)	Jer 24:7; Jer 31:31-40	The promise of a new covenant becomes explicit. Jeremiah chapter 33 (all) links the promise of restoration with the Land and through the line of David. It foretells both the Messiah and a future age of peace and righteousness yet to be seen.
5B	Ezekiel (how)	Ezek 37 (all)	Ezekiel 37 shows how God will bring life from death. The restoration of the Jewish Nation, and through them, the provision of the Messiah of the whole world.
5C	Isaiah (who)	Is 52:13 -53:12	The suffering servant becomes explicit: Is 8:14; 9:1-7; 11:1-5; 32:1-4; 50:2-8; and Is 52:13-53:12; and Is 54 through to 56:8

	Made with	Applies to	Conditionality
0	Adam	Through Adam, applies to all mankind	The conditionality is only spelled out in God's gracious refusal to allow mankind to eat from the tree of life (Gen 3:22)
1	Noah	All mankind	Unconditional
2	Abraham	Through the Hebrews, applies to all mankind	Unconditional
3	Moses	The Hebrews	Conditional on obedience
4	David	David	Unconditional
5	Messianic		
5A	Jeremiah (what)	Through the Hebrews, applies to all mankind	Conditional on obedience
5B	Ezekiel (how)	Through the Hebrews, applies to all mankind	Conditional on obedience
5C	Isaiah (who)	Through the Hebrews, applies to all mankind	Conditional on obedience

APPENDIX 4

This appendix references chapter 6. Verses are taken from the NASV translation.

Old Testament prophecies of the coming Messiah

- And I will put enmity between you and the woman, and between your seed and her seed; He shall bruise you on the head, and you shall bruise him on the heel" (*Genesis 3:15*).
- And I will bless those who bless you, and the one who curses you I will curse. And in you all the families of the earth shall be blessed" (*Genesis 12:3*).
- But God said, "No, but Sarah your wife shall bear you a son, and you shall call his name Isaac; and I will establish My covenant with him for an everlasting covenant for his descendants after him" (*Genesis 17:19*).
- "I see him, but not now; I behold him, but not near; a star shall come forth from Jacob, and a scepter shall rise from Israel, and shall crush through the forehead of Moab, and tear down all the sons of Sheth (*Numbers 24:17*).
- "The scepter shall not depart from Judah, nor the ruler's staff from between his feet, until Shiloh comes, and to him shall be the obedience of the peoples (*Genesis 49:10*).
- Then it will come about in that day that the nations will resort to the root of Jesse, Who will stand as a signal for the peoples; and His resting place will be glorious (*Isaiah 11:10*).
- "Behold, the days are coming," declares the LORD, "When I shall raise up for David a righteous Branch; and He will reign as king and act wisely and do justice and righteousness in the land. In His days Judah will be saved, and Israel will dwell securely; and this is His name by which He will be called, 'The LORD our righteousness'" (*Jeremiah 23:5–6*).

- "And My servant David will be king over them, and they will all have one shepherd; and they will walk in My ordinances, and keep My statutes, and observe them." "They will live on the land that I gave to Jacob My servant, in which your fathers lived; and they will live on it, they, and their sons and their sons' sons, forever; and David My servant will be their prince forever" (*Ezekiel 37:24–25*).

- There will be no end to the increase of His government or of peace, on the throne of David and over his kingdom, to establish it and to uphold it with justice and righteousness from then on and forevermore. The zeal of the LORD of hosts will accomplish this (*Isaiah 9:7*).

- "Behold, My Servant, whom I uphold; My chosen one in whom My soul delights. I have put My Spirit upon Him; He will bring forth justice to the nations. He will not cry out or raise His voice, Nor make His voice heard in the street. A bruised reed He will not break And a dimly burning wick He will not extinguish; He will faithfully bring forth justice. "He will not be disheartened or crushed Until He has established justice in the earth; And the coastlands will wait expectantly for His law." Thus says God the LORD, Who created the heavens and stretched them out, Who spread out the earth and its offspring, Who gives breath to the people on it And spirit to those who walk in it, "I am the LORD, I have called You in righteousness, I will also hold You by the hand and watch over You, And I will appoint You as a covenant to the people, As a light to the nations" (*Isaiah 42:1–6*).

- Thy throne, O God, is forever and ever; A scepter of uprightness is the scepter of Thy kingdom. Thou hast loved righteousness, and hated wickedness; therefore God, Thy God, has anointed Thee with the oil of joy above Thy fellows (*Psalm 45:6–7*).

- "But as for you, Bethlehem Ephrathah, too little to be among the clans of Judah, from you One will go forth for Me to be ruler in Israel. His goings forth are from long ago, from the days of eternity" (*Micah 5:2*).

- "So you are to know and discern that from the issuing of a decree to restore and rebuild Jerusalem until Messiah the Prince there will be seven weeks and sixty-two weeks; it will be built again, with plaza and moat, even in times of distress (*Daniel 9:25*).

- "Therefore the LORD Himself will give you a sign: Behold, a virgin will be with child and bear a son, and she will call His name Immanuel (*Isaiah 7:14*).

- "And nations will come to your light, and kings to the brightness of your rising" (*Isaiah 60:3*).

- When Israel was a youth I loved him, and out of Egypt I called My son (*Hosea 11:1*).

- A voice is calling, "Clear the way for the LORD in the wilderness; make smooth in the desert a highway for our God. Let every valley be lifted up, and every mountain and hill be made low; and let the rough ground become a plain, and the rugged terrain a broad valley; Then the glory of the LORD will be revealed, and all flesh will see it together; for the mouth of the LORD has spoken" (*Isaiah 40:3–5*).

- "Behold, I am going to send My messenger, and he will clear the way before Me. And the LORD, whom you seek, will suddenly come to His temple; and the messenger of the covenant, in whom you delight, behold, He is coming," says the LORD of hosts (*Malachi 3:1*).

- "Behold, I am going to send you Elijah the prophet before the coming of the great and terrible day of the LORD. And he will restore the hearts of the fathers to their children, and the hearts of the children to their fathers, lest I come and smite the land with a curse" (*Malachi 4:5–6*).

- "I will surely tell of the decree of the LORD: He said to Me, 'Thou art My Son, today I have begotten Thee'" (*Psalm 2:7*).

- Who has ascended into heaven and descended? Who has gathered the wind in His fists? Who has wrapped the waters in His garment? Who has established all the ends of the earth? What is His name or His son's name? Surely you know! (*Proverbs 30:4*).
- But there will be no more gloom for her who was in anguish; in earlier times He treated the land of Zebulun and the land of Naphtali with contempt, but later on He shall make it glorious, by the way of the sea, on the other side of Jordan, Galilee of the Gentiles. The people who walk in darkness will see a great light; those who live in a dark land, the light will shine on them (*Isaiah 9:1–2*).
- I will open my mouth in a parable; I will utter dark sayings of old, which we have heard and known, and our fathers have told us. We will not conceal them from their children, but tell to the generation to come the praises of the LORD, and His strength and His wondrous works that He has done (*Psalm 78:2–4*).
- "The LORD your God will raise up for you a prophet like me from among you, from your countrymen, you shall listen to him" (*Deuteronomy 18:15*).
- And on that day the deaf shall hear words of a book, and out of their gloom and darkness the eyes of the blind shall see (*Isaiah 29:18*).
- Then the eyes of the blind will be opened, and the ears of the deaf will be unstopped. Then the lame will leap like a deer, and the tongue of the dumb will shout for joy. For waters will break forth in the wilderness and streams in the Arabah (*Isaiah 35:5–6*).
- "He will not cry out or raise His voice, Nor make His voice heard in the street. "A bruised reed He will not break, and a dimly burning wick He will not extinguish; He will faithfully bring forth justice. (*Isaiah 42:2-3*)
- He was oppressed and He was afflicted, Yet He did not open His mouth; like a lamb that is led to slaughter, and like a sheep that is silent before its shearers, so He did

not open His mouth (*Isaiah 53:7*).

- Listen to Me, O islands, and pay attention, you peoples from afar. The LORD called Me from the womb; from the body of My mother He named Me (*Isaiah 49:1*).
- The Spirit of the LORD God is upon me, because the LORD has anointed me to bring good news to the afflicted; He has sent me to bind up the brokenhearted, to proclaim liberty to captives, and freedom to prisoners; to proclaim the favourable year of the LORD, and the day of vengeance of our God; to comfort all who mourn... (*Isaiah 61:1–2*).
- Therefore, I will allot Him a portion with the great, And He will divide the booty with the strong; Because He poured out Himself to death, and was numbered with the transgressors; Yet He Himself bore the sin of many, and interceded for the transgressors (*Isaiah 53:12*).
- And He saw that there was no man, and was astonished that there was no one to intercede; Then His own arm brought salvation to Him; And His righteousness upheld Him (*Isaiah 59:16*).

This appendix references chapter 6.
Verses are taken from the NASV translation.

Old Testament prophecies concerning the Hebrew People

(1) And I will make you a great nation, And I will bless you, And make your name great; And so you shall be a blessing; And I will bless those who bless you, And the one who curses you I will curse. And in you all the families of the earth will be blessed." (*Genesis 12:2-3*)

(2) "For you are a holy people to the LORD your God; the LORD your God has chosen you to be a people for His own possession out of all the peoples who are on the face of the earth. (*Deuteronomy 7:6*)

(3) Blessed is the nation whose God is the LORD, The people whom He has chosen for His own inheritance. (*Psalm 33:12*)

But chose the tribe of Judah, Mount Zion which He loved. And He built His sanctuary like the heights, Like the earth which He has founded forever. He also chose David His servant And took him from the sheepfolds; From the care of the ewes with suckling lambs He brought him To shepherd Jacob His people, And Israel His inheritance. So he shepherded them according to the integrity of his heart, And guided them with his skilful hands. (*Psalm 78:68-72*)

"I have made a covenant with My chosen; I have sworn to David My servant, I will establish your seed forever And build up your throne to all generations." (*Psalm 89:3-4*)

O seed of Abraham, His servant, O sons of Jacob, His chosen ones! (*Psalm 105:6*)

For the LORD has chosen Jacob for Himself, Israel for His own possession. (*Psalm 135:4*)

"But you, Israel, My servant, Jacob whom I have chosen, Descendant of Abraham My friend, You whom I have taken from the ends of the earth, And called from its remotest parts

And said to you, 'You are My servant, I have chosen you and not rejected you." (*Isaiah 41:9*)

(4) "Yet on your fathers did the LORD set His affection to love them, and He chose their descendants after them, even you above all peoples, as it is this day. So circumcise your heart, and stiffen your neck no longer. For the LORD your God is the God of gods and the Lord of lords, the great, the mighty, and the awesome God who does not show partiality nor take a bribe. He executes justice for the orphan and the widow, and shows His love for the alien by giving him food and clothing. So show your love for the alien, for you were aliens in the land of Egypt." (*Deuteronomy 10:19*)

(5) "Know, then, it is not because of your righteousness that the LORD your God is giving you this good land to possess, for you are a stubborn people. (*Deuteronomy 9:6*)

(6) A voice is calling, "Clear the way for the LORD in the wilderness; make smooth in the desert a highway for our God. Let every valley be lifted up, and every mountain and hill be made low; and let the rough ground become a plain, and the rugged terrain a broad valley; Then the glory of the LORD will be revealed, and all flesh will see it together; for the mouth of the LORD has spoken." (*Isaiah 40:3-5*) For a child will be born to us, a son will be given to us; And the government will rest on His shoulders; And His name will be called Wonderful Counsellor, Mighty God, Eternal Father, Prince of Peace. (*Isaiah 9:6*) "Behold, the days are coming," declares the LORD, "When I shall raise up for David a righteous Branch; and He will reign as king and act wisely and do justice and righteousness in the land. In His days Judah will be saved, and Israel will dwell securely; and this is His name by which He will be called, `The LORD our righteousness.'" (*Jeremiah 23:5-6*) Thy throne, O God, is forever and ever; A scepter of uprightness is the scepter of Thy kingdom. Thou hast loved righteousness, and hated wickedness; therefore God, Thy God, has anointed Thee with the oil of joy above Thy fellows. (*Psalm 45:6-7*)

The LORD says to my Lord: "Sit at My right hand, until I make Thine enemies a footstool for Thy feet." (*Psalm 110:1*) "But as for you, Bethlehem Ephrathah, too little to be among the clans of Judah, from you One will go forth for Me to be ruler in Israel. His goings forth are from long ago, from the days of eternity." (*Micah 5:2*)

(7) "I will surely tell of the decree of the LORD: He said to Me, `Thou art My Son, today I have begotten Thee.'" (*Psalm 2:7*) Who has ascended into heaven and descended? Who has gathered the wind in His fists? Who has wrapped the waters in His garment? Who has established all the ends of the earth? What is His name or His son's name? Surely you know! (*Proverbs 30:4*)

(8) "Incline your ear and come to Me. Listen, that you may live; And I will make an everlasting covenant with you, According to the faithful mercies shown to David. Behold, I have made him a witness to the peoples, a leader and commander for the peoples. (*Isaiah 55:3-4*) Behold, days are coming," declares the LORD, "when I will make a new covenant with the house of Israel and with the house of Judah,...But this is the covenant which I will make with the house of Israel after those days," declares the LORD, "I will put My law within them, and on their heart I will write it; and I will be their God, and they shall be My people. (*Jeremiah 31:31*)

(9) But He was pierced through for our transgressions, He was crushed for our iniquities; The chastening for our well-being fell upon Him, and by His scourging we are healed. (*Isaiah 53:5*) Therefore, I will allot Him a portion with the great, And He will divide the booty with the strong; Because He poured out Himself to death, And was numbered with the transgressors; Yet He Himself bore the sin of many, And interceded for the transgressors. (*Isaiah 53:12*) And He saw that there was no man, And was astonished that there was no one to intercede; Then His own arm brought salvation to Him; And His righteousness upheld Him. (*Isaiah 59:16*)

"And I will pour out on the house of David and on the inhabitants of Jerusalem, the Spirit of grace and of supplication, so that they will look on Me whom they have pierced; and they will mourn for Him, as one mourns for an only son, and they will weep bitterly over Him, like the bitter weeping over a first-born. (*Zechariah 12:10*) For dogs have surrounded me; A band of evildoers has encompassed me; They pierced my hands and my feet. (*Psalm 22:16*)

APPENDIX 6

THE ROADS TO APOSTASY
An extract from
The Bible Student[1]

Background

The word 'apostasy' derives from the Greek *apostasia* which means to 'withdraw' or to 'fall away' (2 Thessalonians 2:3). Today it is used to mean the abandonment by a professing Christian of the fundamental principles of the Christian gospel. History shows that apostasy does not generally come into the church as a single event. Its encroachment is gradual and insidious. All Christians therefore need to be aware of the 'roads' that lead to apostasy, alert to the possibility of treading those roads themselves, and prepared to help others to see the danger. The short letter of Jude in the New Testament warns about this dreadful danger. The Holy Bible identifies at least three dangerous 'roads':

1. The 'way of Cain' (Jude 11), i.e. a 'bloodless' religion, that rejects in some way the full Bible teaching on the Cross;
2. The 'error of Balaam' (Jude 11), i.e. compromise with the world;
3. The 'teaching of the Nicolaitans' – compromise with the world, but especially with other religions.

There are surely other paths that lead away from 'the Way' (Acts 24:14, 22) but these three above seem to have beset Christ's church from the very beginning. We examine them in greater detail below:

The Way of Cain

This applies when a Christian seeks a way of forgiveness of his sins by any other means than cleansing through the blood of Jesus. The idea that we can be forgiven by our 'good works' is perhaps the most insidious and pervasive example; or, through the intellect, to believe that Jesus is an 'example' that we should strive to follow in our own strength, but not feel too disheartened when we fail! This is perhaps the key outcome of 'modernism' or 'liberalism' wherever it is encountered in the church of Christ – it certainly seems to have made real headway in the organised church in the twentieth century. An apparently opposed form of the error – that of Cain – is those religious people (and we have in mind here people within the Christian church) who may be trusting in their religious profession or their 'zeal' for God, whilst sin remains unsurrendered and uncleansed in their hearts. The zealot and the extreme liberal are often closer than either of them would like to admit!

If we understand the biblical account of Cain (Genesis 4) correctly, it seems that Cain found no peace with God, and then looked in anger at his brother whose sacrifice had been found acceptable to God. Anger can be a sign that sin remains uncleansed. Not only individuals, but also whole Christian communities can tread the 'way of Cain'. We think then of extreme liberal 'churches' with no vital message – or strictly orthodox ones, but often riven with internal dissension and jealousy.

Genesis 4:1–5 (Hebrews 11: 4); Acts 15:1, 2, 19, 24; 20:30; 2 Corinthians 11:3; Galatians 1:6–9; 2:11–16; 3:1–4; 6:12–15; Philippians 3:18, 19 (the perversion of the cross of Christ into a license for sin); Colossians 2:16, 17, 20–23 (adding non-essentials to the gospel); 2 Timothy 4:3–4; 2 Peter 2:1–2; 14–15; 2 John 7; Jude 3, 4 and 11.

The Way of Balaam
For the Christian this implies compromise with the world. (2 Peter 2:15). It is clear from the account in the book of Numbers that this prophet-for-hire failed God in two ways: He desired to make a market of his divine gift (Numbers 22:12, 18, 19). Although in the end he reluctantly complied

with God's commands (the right decision), he seemed to look for a change of heart in God that might bring him material rewards.

He taught the Israelites to defile themselves with heathen practices (Numbers 25:1–3; 31:16).

For the Christian disciple, Balaam's way represents any 'sharp practice' with money, or of making the Lord's service a way to worldly advancement or gain. It also represents worldliness, when the soul is no longer satisfied with the Lordship of Jesus, and so satisfaction from the world is sought. The result is a church infected by this worldly spirit, and accordingly resorting to worldly methods (e.g. raising money via lottery) or dependence on the arm of flesh (e.g. asking for State handouts so as to be able to perform 'good works'). At one extreme, parts of the church seem to think they are an extension of the social services. For a time such methods may appear to succeed, but there is an inevitable loss of spiritual vitality and an increasing deadness in ministry.

Matthew 7:15; Luke 16:13; 2 Corinthians 11:13–15; 1 Timothy 6:5, 10; 2 Timothy 3:5; 2 Peter 2:17, 20–21; Jude 11, 16.

The Teaching of the Nicolaitans

The Nicolaitans were a heretical sect of the very early church mentioned twice in the book of Revelation. (Revelation 2:6, 15). Amongst some 'Christian' sects is found 'priestcraft' and religious domination in different ways. This is an intrusion of a man-made priesthood. Jesus the Christ is our high priest and has opened up a way for all believers that is independent of any human agency. At its worst, this priestcraft tries to divide the body of Christ into priests and laity, and to put the 'priests' into the position of mediators between man and God. The effect is that both 'priest' and people tend to lose faith in Christ alone and instead put their faith in ceremonial and outward forms. There are many warnings of this and it does seem that in the end times, an apostate 'Christendom' will be reunited under one supreme head (and possibly united with other religions). The Bible calls this person *the* antichrist as he will set himself up as a Messiah of some sort.

Priestly domination seems to lead invariably to religious persecution.

Isaiah 1:4–6; 13–15; 5:5–7; Ezekiel 8:9–16 (idolatry in the House of the Lord); Colossians 2:20–23; 1 Timothy 2:5; 4:1–3.

In Conclusion

Believers in the true Messiah, Jesus, are to be alert to the temptation from our enemy to turn away from the salvation journey on which we are embarked. The warnings are sufficiently frequent, both in the Old and the New Testaments, that we cannot avoid the conclusion that we are being given *real and urgent* warnings. It would be foolish to ignore these. The illusion of self-earned salvation, the temptations of the world, and the imposition of false religiousness are each real and dangerous errors to avoid. Christians should prayerfully be aware of these, on the watch for them, and gently seek to help others who may be in danger of falling into them.

[1] *The Bible Student* see Further Reading.

FURTHER READING

Most of these books remain available commercially. All are recommended.

CHURCH AND STATE IN THE NEW MILLENNIUM – issues of belief and morality for the 21st century
David Holloway, (Harper Collins, 2000)

THE CHURCH IN CRISIS
David N Samuel, [The Church of England (Continuing) 2004] (Available via www.cofec.org)

BECOMING A CITIZEN OF THE KINGDOM
Patrick Whitworth, (TerraNova Publications, 2006)

READY OR NOT – HE IS COMING
Stephanie Cottam, (Glory to Glory Publications, 2012)

UNDERSTANDING REVELATION – a preacher looks at the end-time message of the last book of the Bible
Paul Langham, (Terra Nova Publications, 2005)

THE EMPTY PROMISE OF GODISM – reflections on the multi-faith agenda
Peter Sammons, (Glory to Glory Publications, 2009)

THE BIBLE STUDENT – fifty key themes explored through the Holy Bible, multi-authored, (Glory to Glory Publications, 2012) (available worldwide via Amazon).

THE BISHOP'S NEW CLOTHES Steve Maltz (Saffron Planet, 2013).

HOW THE CHURCH LOST THE WAY – and how it can find it again, Steve Maltz (Saffron Planet, 2009).

HOW THE CHURCH LOST THE TRUTH – and how it can find it again, Steve Maltz (Saffron Planet, 2010).

TO LIFE – Rediscovering Biblical Church, Steve Maltz, (Saffron Planet 2011)

[These three books are also available as an extended home group study course with study guide. The course is entitled CHURCH LOST AND FOUND – also available via Saffron Planet, together with three DVD disks:
www.sppublishing.com]

WHAT IS AN EVANGELICAL?
David Martyn Lloyd-Jones, (Banner of Truth Trust, 1992)

ONE NEW MAN BIBLE
Hebrew Scriptures Edited and Greek NT Text
trans. William J Morford (True Potential Publishing, Inc.,
USA, 2011)
ISRAEL IN THE NEW TESTAMENT
David Pawson (Terra Nova Publications International, 2009)
DEFENDING CHRISTIAN ZIONISM
David Pawson (Anchor Recordings, revised 2013)
RECEIVE THE TRUTH
(20 FAQs and 10 Bible Talks focusing on key issues in
contemporary Christian-Jewish relations and Christian
Spirituality) Alex Jacob, (Glory to Glory, 2011)
THE CASE FOR ENLARGEMENT THEOLOGY
(2nd Edition) Alex Jacob, (Glory to Glory, 2011)